CW00384934

Apricot Dumplings

A Guided Tour around my Home

Ilma Scantlebury

Printed in Great Britain by Amazon

Contents

Acknowledgements

Writing my family history was a labour of love and it took a long time. Many people helped me along the way with sound advice and encouragement. In particular, I am grateful to Karen Clark, Margaret Ives, Derek and Margaret Jewel, Jane Kingsbury, Natalie Marshall and Fiona Thomas.

István Matievics was my 'Hungarian conscience'; with mathematical precision he checked dates and historical facts. Andrew Scantlebury, Julia Blundell and Keith Wilson were my supportive 'sounding board', listening to every freshly written chunk.

Once it was written, Michael Scantlebury and Brigid Callaghan did a thorough pre-edit, to ensure that the text makes sense for an English speaking audience.

Karen Perkins, my lovely editor, guided me through the bewildering process of getting the work ready for publishing. She did this with kindness, patience and utter professionalism.

For the front cover, Liz Scantlebury painted the wonderful *A Tree of Life* and presented me with the original. For all your kindness, patience and support I am truly grateful. Thank you all.

For all past, present and future members of my family

A Hungarian in Cambridge

The year was 1964. The Beatles had just released *A Hard Day's Night*, but *Sgt Pepper's Lonely Hearts Club Band* did not exist as yet. Imagine!

West and East Europe were still firmly divided. Hungary belonged to the Soviet-occupied Eastern communist bloc. But something unexpected and wonderful happened to me when I was halfway through my studies at the University of Budapest. Out of the blue, my father's brother, who lived in Toronto, offered to pay for a course organised by Cambridge University for foreign students studying English in their own countries. At the time, travel to the West was almost impossible for us, passports difficult to get, the $5 daily allowance pitiful and the course fees in Cambridge, with full board and lodging, astronomical. Of course I jumped at the chance.

Accepting the generous offer was the easy part. I made my way through Europe by train, navigated through London, got to Cambridge and found the allocated address in Parkside, where I was to stay. So far so good.

Good old Mr and Mrs Tupling rented their upstairs rooms to undergraduates in term time and to foreign students in the summer. I joined four girls: a Greek, a Norwegian and two French. But I soon found that I was way out of my league. The French were impossibly well groomed, with elegant and obviously expensive clothes, the Greek had a wealth of tinkley jewellery and what the Norwegian girl lacked in elegance and jewellery she more than made up for with a barefooted, joyous ease and impeccable English. Oh dear!

The course induction wasn't much better either. A Babel of languages around me, no other Hungarian, everyone self-assured. 'Right,' I said to myself in the evening, as I munched alone on what was left of my now dry and wrinkled bread rolls from home, 'you are obviously going to be pretty lonely here, but you came to learn and that is what you are going to do. And, meanwhile,' looking at the crumpled heap of my clothes, 'there is no need to look untidy.'

Down I wander with my bundle in search of Mrs Tupling. 'I want to press.' She looks at me, bewildered. 'Press!' I repeat, louder, shoving my creased dresses towards her. Light dawns on her face: 'She wants an iron!' (Hungarian textbooks please note: The English usually say: to iron, an iron or an ironing board, only rarely press!)

While I was ironing I asked her advice about where I should go in Cambridge, what I should see, what is it that I mustn't miss? The Colleges, she said, which didn't seem much use to me. I was disappointed. Next morning though, as I was coming down the stairs, there was a lad in the hall, struggling with a trunk of books.

'This is David, one of our boys,' she said, by way of introduction, 'he will show you Cambridge.' He did, that evening, and the evening after and after. My confusion about 'one of our boys' was soon cleared up. He wasn't Mrs Tupling's son, but one of their term-time lodgers. His subject required that he spent the 'long-vac term' in the summer on lab work, and he had to stay in Downing College, hence the collecting of books.

There was a lot to see. There were the colleges, each a delight. The fish shop on Petty Cury. I had never seen sea fish before. All the amazing shapes, even flat ones! And then of course the two dishes with whiskery creatures, with an awful lot of legs, prawns and shrimps. I couldn't believe people actually ate them. David got me a few ounces of each, in paper bags, just to try; and boy, were they delicious! Bless him; he also got us tickets to a concert in Saint John's College Chapel. It didn't seem a big deal because concerts and theatres were very cheap in Hungary, so when he asked whether I wanted to go to a Brahms concert I said 'sure, why not.' It was a wonderful concert, but I only found out years later that those tickets practically bankrupted him.

Not everything went to plan. He asked whether I wanted to see the boat races. I vaguely knew that Cambridge was associated with them, so I said yes. What shall I wear, was my next problem. I put on my lovely, short white linen skirt, a little top, white high heels, and was ready to lean on David's arm by the Cam and languidly watch one or two boats drifting by.

David arrived wheeling his bike. That was strange. 'Sit here on the bank,' he said. And that was almost the last I saw of him. The rest was just a blur, as he occasionally whizzed by me, but oblivious of my presence, yelling, 'Come on, Downing.' Two hours later he returned. Somebody must have won, I suppose, but I didn't care. 'How am I going to get these grass stains out?' was my only concern.

We talked, wandered, discovered, and watched the moon, looking down on us. David repeatedly had to climb into College. In those days they locked the college gates at 10, by which time everyone was supposed to be in and alone, definitely no females!

I was getting uneasy. *This boy is getting far too keen*, I felt. I didn't want him to get hurt. So I told him: 'I'll never marry a foreigner.' Quick as a flash came the riposte: 'Don't worry, I haven't asked you,' and I felt so ashamed. But it was important to me that I am Hungarian and I felt, that because we are so few, only 10 million, we have a duty to stay in Hungary.

Meanwhile I missed quite a few lectures. We were

presented with a veritable smorgasbord; on the menu were English phonemes, Shakespeare's dramas, syntax and *Beowulf* as I remember. I suppose they were the pet topics of the various lecturers, and some of them were interesting, but nowhere near as interesting as spending time with David.

The other girls noticed my absences. When they learned that I was going out with a real life English undergraduate they reacted as one: 'Where did you find him?' That's when I became aware of an understanding clear to all of them, except myself. To paraphrase Jane Austen: every young man in possession of a Cambridge degree and prospects of a glittering career is in need of a wife. (Preferably Norwegian, Greek or French, they reckoned.) To be fair, the Norwegian girl did secure a Jack from Trinity.

Two weeks after my embarrassing declaration, David did ask me to marry him and by that time I did not say no. It was six weeks in all, that first trip to England, and my life changed forever. For a start, my English language skills made a quantum leap. We were sure what we wanted but it wasn't easy.

I insisted that I leave my country legally and a petition took a year to run its course. I also had two more years at university; there was no question in my mind of not finishing it. So we wrote letters for a whole year.

Next summer he came to Hungary and we got

married there in order to apply for permission to leave as a Hungarian citizen, living abroad. Two years after we met I joined him in England and had a 'blessing of a marriage' ceremony in Cornwall, in a little woodland church.

Both set of parents reacted the same way. 'Couldn't you find a nice Hungarian boy?' said my mother, raising her hands to her face in shock, when I told her about our decision. David's parents had the same question: 'What's wrong with Cornish girls?'

Miss Dennis, David's mother's best friend had a serious concern. 'Can she crimp a pasty?' she wanted to know. I didn't know what a pasty was, let alone crimp it somehow, but learned soon enough, as is the duty of anyone marrying a Cornishman.

That concert, 1964

In a punt, 1964

David and me, 1964

England is my Home

Here I married, loved, had my three children, worked, paid my taxes, laughed and grieved, and along the way made many close relationships. I gathered fifty-three-years' worth of memories and people to love.

But the first twenty-one years of my life were spent in Hungary. My early, defining memories and the language I first spoke are Hungarian. Because I had the extraordinary good fortune to be able to travel freely between the two countries, the old, intimate family bonds and friendships continued unbroken. They are as alive now as they were fifty-odd years ago. I have many people and places to love in Hungary, too.

I have two homes, equally precious, if we call 'home' where we have people to love. There is something strange about this swapping country and language business. I experience it as a noticeable mental shift whenever I travel to the 'other' country. When I am in Britain, Hungary seems but a distant memory. I look at 'them' with English eyes. I see the national idiosyncrasies, the achievements and failures, and marvel at the complexity, versatility and the sheer alienness of the language, the lack of similarities to anything in Europe.

But as soon as I touch down at Budapest airport I switch; my existence in Manchester becomes a shadow, just a remembered life. The planeload of British tourists become 'them' and I watch, with the mild disdain of the local, the bewildered, earnest middle-aged couple clinging to the guidebook, or the noisy group of hen party girls, in crazy tee-shirts, ready for some fun.

Like most of the locals I get on the 200E bus and listen to the bilingual announcement that it will terminate at Kőbánya Kispest metro station. I am somewhat astonished that I understand every word of the English. How did that happen? I change to the metro, the familiar stations roll by. Ecseri út, my favourite flea market, Nagyvárad tér, where my dentist was, Kálvin tér, where I first stayed in a hotel with my mother at the age of ten and Ferenciek tere. Here I used to know every single café when I was a student; we spent many an hour solving the world's problems over an espresso coffee. I change for a bus, just a few stops now across the Danube, offering me the world's most magnificent sight, the stately river, the series of elegant bridges, parliament on the Pest side, the imposing bulk of the castle in Buda and the hills, the hills, receding far into the distance. Home.

I bought my flat in Budapest when my mother, the last of her generation, died. From my parents' belongings my sister and I chose items dear to us. Family and friends helped and took whatever they had a use for; but I was still left with enough to sparsely furnish my new flat. Now the desk, the chairs, the bed are all here, all alive, in harmony with each other, still carefully polished and dusted. Yet the people who once touched them are long gone. It is about the lives of these people that I write.

These pieces are messengers of times gone by, haphazardly washed up by the many tides of history. Saxa loquuntur, the Latin says, 'The stones speak,' but how much louder these few sticks talk to me, recalling events and emotions still on the edge of living memory.

Looking at these things, thinking about them and thinking about the fate of those who owned them before me has filled me with intense pleasure and wonder. While I have been writing, I had the feeling that I was a guide of some space and time travel agency, taking my listeners to places and times where our past was still their vivid present.

Like beads on a necklace I thread the life stories of members of my family, connected with their own time and their items, and find to my own great astonishment, that it makes a coherent story, a story of a daisy chain of lives, worth remembering and yes, worth celebrating.

We were, and are, ordinary in many ways. Not one hero, no revolutionary poet, no Olympic athlete amongst us, at least not in the past 200 or so years, the time span I feel I can recreate with some measure of truth. 'A drop contains the ocean,' my father used to say. Though the path of just this one family might be singular, it is still a mirror of many, many more around them at those times and in those places.

I relied on my own memory of events and the memory of those who told and retold me their stories. I am also wary, knowing how memory distorts, reinterprets and colludes with our self-image. Luckily, I also have diaries, photographs and letters to keep me somewhere near to what could be called a version of 'truth'.

I am not writing a novel, so don't look for a continuous series of events, don't look for a central character and subsidiary ones. All the people I write about are equally important because they all lived. They lived and died, each complete, self-contained, each a beautiful shiny sphere and the thread which connects them is kinship. However, times merge because lifespans overlap. So instead of settling down and reading a novel, imagine that you are visiting me in my Budapest apartment, you look around, you take in the bits and pieces, I offer you some food and the stories begin. 'You see my desk? Well, it was like this...'

'And this chair you are sitting on. My great-great-great-grandfather sat in it once.'

We roam far and wide; centuries roll by and

magically the 'here and there', the 'then and now' merge.

Now, as anyone knows, a Space and Time Travel Agency, like this one, will need to have a name, wishing to evoke trust, a sense of reliability and even fun. A memorable, mysterious kind of name which nevertheless does not contradict the trade's description act. 'Perpetual Sunshine' would be untrue, 'Turbulent Times' off-putting.

Let the company – my story – be called: Apricot Dumplings! And if you don't know how delicious those are, read on!

Hungarians

Before we start and I serve you those lovely dumplings, I need to give my English speaking readers a 'crash course' on what it means to be Hungarian. I realised that this was necessary when an English friend of mine read some of the sections while I was putting the chapters together. Her comment was: 'I don't understand. People just don't behave the way you described.'

Well, they did, but the reasons why they would choose those paths seemed entirely hidden from her. Of course it isn't possible to describe the ever-changing phenomenon of a nation or to reduce the complexities to just a few sentences. Nevertheless, I am going to try to give a few pointers to my non-Hungarian readers.

Let's start with some local, fond imaginings. It is said, in Hungary, that Hungarian women are the most beautiful in the world – as well as passionate, fiery and intriguing. I am Hungarian, I am female and who am I to argue with this statement? I have a sneaking suspicion, though, that there isn't a nation on Earth who would not contest this opinion and praise their own womenfolk above all others.

We would also like to believe that our cooking is world famous. This happens to be mentioned to many a gullible foreign visitor. Well, I do appreciate a good 'gulyás' (soup of the cowboy) and a nice sour dough loaf to go with it, as much as the next Hungarian, but step outside the borders and our world-wide fame seems to evaporate.

It is another cliché that our language is impossible to learn for a foreigner. Not quite true, of course, but it is true that it is not Indo-European and has nothing in common with English, French, Italian, Spanish, Russian, Polish, Swedish, Greek or any other European tongue, apart from being vaguely related to Finnish and Estonian. Not only are our words incomprehensible to a foreigner, so is the whole grammatical structure. This in itself is interesting, but mainly for a linguist.

Many people have argued that language and thought are a two-way process. Thought influences language, and language in turn influences thinking and perception. Some (Hungarian) authors maintained that our surprisingly numerous national achievements in the fields of science, mathematics and music are the result of the extraordinarily logical structure of our native tongue. These achievements could, of course, have something to do with schools and national aspirations.

Whatever else the effects of this unique language

might be, it is certainly true that it is isolating, it is a barrier between us and all other Europeans around us. We feel different, we feel alone, like an only child longingly looking at other children who have so many brothers and sisters and so many cousins.

More important than the language is our history. It is believed that the pagan Hungarian tribes occupied the Carpathian Basin in the 9th century, took up Christianity in the year 1000 and established a large and powerful kingdom for the next 500 years. On the 29th of August 1526, however, the Hungarian army suffered a crushing defeat against Suleiman the Great's Muslim army, our king died in battle and a 150-year-long Turkish occupation followed. Of course we fought back. We tried, we struggled, we played politics, forged alliances and engaged in intrigues. The intervening centuries of Hungarian history are littered with failed attempts. The vast Hungarian Empire of the 15th century is but a glorious memory. Up until the present, for the past 500 years, we have not won a single war.

Hungarian history timeline:

13th century onwards, attacking Ottoman Empire an ever-present threat.

1526 at Mohács Hungary suffered a final defeat, resulting in a continuous expansion of Ottoman territories till 1557.

1699 Combined Austrian and European efforts

defeated the Ottomans and the whole of Hungary was ruled from Austria.

From 1526 till 1699 the country was in political chaos. Rival factions had elected two kings, the Hungarian Zápolya and the Austrian Hapsburg, Ferdinand.

This meant that the West of Hungary was ruled by Austria, and was therefore Catholic. The central regions were occupied by the Ottomans, and the East and Transylvania were first under Hungarian rule and later became a vassal state of the Ottoman Empire. The Central and Eastern territories were largely Protestant, and belligerently Hungarian speaking as a mark of defiance to the Hapsburg rule. Our Anthem mirrors the deep-seated national sadness. The words, which only we can understand, are a prayer: 'God bless the Hungarians... Protect us from our enemies for we have already been punished enough for the past and for our future.' If the words are devoid of hope, the tune, slow and solemn, like a funeral march, does nothing to mitigate it either.

Our other national song follows in the same vein. 'Be true to your country, oh Hungarian, This is your cradle and your grave... You must live and die here.' The tune is also funereal, only rising to a triumphant crescendo at the last words: YOU MUST DIE HERE.

I, like most of my compatriots, sing our anthem as tears sting my eyes. We stand, ramrod straight. It is loyalty, belonging and respect.

I can't help wondering, though, whether it was a wise decision in the 19th century to adopt this particular anthem. If you had a child would you consciously and continually tell that child: 'Well, little Johnny, ill fortune has haunted all your kin, their lot in life was suffering. What's more, you too have to stay here whatever happens and endure till the day you die.' With what kind of a self-image would little Johnny grow up?

Would he look at all the 'others' and doggedly try to outdo them within his chosen field? Would he give up and complain? Or would he just leave the country and try his luck in another? Currently all three responses are amply represented.

If a country was a commodity, hence subject of an advertising campaign, would you try to 'sell' it by saying that you are guaranteed to have a tough time here, that God alone can help you because you are surely incapable of helping yourself?

Other nations were perhaps more astute than us, with a much more positive self-image. I am not just thinking of the 'big boys,' like 'land of the free and home of the brave' (USA) 'We are millions ... March on, March on! Charge!' (China). France, with her *Marseillaise*, Britain's 'Victorious, happy and glorious' or Russia's 'A mighty will, great glory, these are yours for all time.'

It is easy for them, they were the winners, we might say from the pit of the Hungarian misery. Not so. The Danes were mighty once, so were the Swedes and Portuguese, yet in thinking about themselves they all preserved pride and joy. The two Northerners rejoice in their land and people, and the Portuguese see themselves still as 'heroes of the sea, noble race, immortal nation.'

We Hungarians have our own National Anthem and we love it as it is. Nobody is suggesting that we should replace it. But if we could find our own equivalent of the English *Jerusalem*, something affirmative and cheery, it would perhaps make a better national mantra.

So we tend to oscillate between wild hope and deep depression, futile bravery and lassitude. All we can claim as an achievement is that we are still here, though dwindling in numbers. Try to explain our mentality to a British person who sang *Rule Britannia* merrily since early childhood, secure in the belief that 'Britons never, never shall be slaves!'

I found this scrutiny of our national psyche difficult to write. But it is the truth, as I see it. An acknowledgement of weak points is painful, because I think we would all like to believe that we are wonderful in every respect. But only by facing our deficiencies can we move forward to something more stable and joyous. I hope that if I can explain to my non-Hungarian readers what the hidden handicaps are, or were, perhaps they can read the life stories of my people with a clearer understanding.

The Waistcoat

In my flat, tucked away in a box, there is a child's waistcoat. It is folded but utterly ragged and useless; it barely ever sees the light of day. I didn't even know that it still existed until I found it amongst my mother's possessions, next to her withered wedding bouquet. It was mine once. This is my story; and there, by the grace of God, goeth I.

Fresh snow muffled the sounds in the ancient North Eastern frontier town of Hungary, Ungvár. This is the place where the conquering Hungarian tribes established their first stronghold, giving us the name outside our boundaries: Hungary. 'Ungarn' meaning the people whose castle is on the Ung River. We call ourselves Magyar.

In the far distance, the majestic peaks of the Carpathians glistened in the brilliant winter sun. All was still, only the graceful arches of the fir trees nodded gently under their sparkling burden. It was 1943, 10 o'clock in the morning, on this last Advent Sunday before Christmas, and a church bell started. Soon others joined in, tinkling, booming, clanging, and shattering the calm of the crystal-clear air.

Fervent human voices of the various congregations sang, 'Peace on Earth and Goodwill to all Mankind.'

I was born into all this clamour and frosty splendour, the first child of Dr Dezső Gyüre and his wife, Ilma Reinbold.

My mother thought that I was the most beautiful thing that ever saw the light of day; my father checked that I had the requisite number of fingers and toes and was satisfied; the visiting well-wishers quietly agreed that this was one peculiar looking infant, with its nose starting right from its forehead. But it was not a particularly safe time to get born, not in Ungvár, not in the December of 1943. Rarely has 'Peace on Earth and Goodwill to all Mankind' been sung with such heartfelt longing because all around us was turmoil; we were at war and the fighting armies were getting ever closer. I was entering a murderous, uncertain world.

A closer look at the political situation of the time from a Hungarian perspective will instantly reveal just how precarious existence was for all. Hungary is geographically in the middle of Europe, bordered by Germany and Austria to the west and our great enemy, the Soviet Empire, to the east of us. Their war had nothing to do with us and, after all the losses of the first Great War, Hungary wished to avoid involvement at all costs in the Second World War.

While politicians argued amongst themselves, wondering which alliance would be the most beneficial for the country, the population tried to interpret the news, such as it was, on radio, in newspapers and rumours, the kind of 'I heard it from a most reliable source...' It was an anxious time for everyone.

We now know that in fact the Regent, Head of State Miklós Horthy conducted secret armistice negotiations with both the United States and the United Kingdom. He was trying his best to keep us out of the war, but fears became a reality in 1940 when Hungary was forced by Germany to join 'the Axis' (the alliance of Germany, Italy and Japan), and was ordered to participate in the invasion of the Soviet Union as part of the Axis army.

Hungarian losses were very heavy throughout the campaign, as expected of this hopelessly futile mission. The final blow came in January 1943 when the Russians annihilated the Hungarian army at the Don River. Encircled and forced into open terrain in the extreme cold (-30/40°C) they were slaughtered. The Armoured Division had a single tank left and the Air Group died on the ground. Of the 200,000 strong Hungarian army and 50,000 Hungarian Jewish labour battalions, 100,000 were dead, 35,000 wounded and 60,000 were taken as prisoners of war. It was said that 'No nation had lost as much blood during World War II in such a short period of time.' By the end of the war from the 10 million Hungarian population, 430,000 died. Compare this with the United Kingdom's losses, from the 48 million people 450,000 died. Our losses were almost equal in numbers, yet the population was only one fifth of the UK.

The Axis powers could not stop the advancing Russian army after January 1943. Ungvár was always an Eastern frontier town. Defeat followed defeat and the front became dangerously close.

And this was the time I decided to enter the world!

My father came to an agonising decision. He didn't dare to expose his wife and baby daughter to danger. He reckoned that we would be safer staying with his mother. But this meant giving up their home. Tearfully they packed up everything they owned, took whatever they could, and the rest of their possessions were left in safekeeping with trusted friends who opted to stay. While it was relatively safe, my father still worked at Ungvár hospital because he was reluctant to relinquish his duty.

The decision to leave was proved right; Ungvár indeed was occupied by the Russian army and was never again returned to Hungary. It belongs to the Ukraine today, now called Usgorod, and with that our little family acquired a new status: we became 'displaced citizens'.

Worse was to follow. Hungary had no army to speak of, and in March 1944 the Nazi army occupied Hungary. Horthy was replaced by the fascist leader Szálasi.

I was only a few months old when my mother and

I arrived to Tiszaderzs, a tiny hamlet in the heart of the Great Hungarian Lowlands. This is where my father was born and where his mother still lived. Within a few months, my father joined us, because by this time the Russians had advanced well into Hungary and the front was near again. Go or stay?

They felt they had to flee. So, off they all moved again, burdened down not only with me but my aged grandmother. Nowhere was it safe, which way would the Russians go? What the Germans would do was anybody's guess. How to avoid them both, how not to get caught in the centre when they would clash; the question was literally – to be or not to be.

Our family wasn't the only one on the move. Other displaced, homeless Hungarians from areas now occupied were also fleeing. We were all put on a train, moving west, just ahead of the front. Avoiding Budapest, along the Danube we made our slow way, occasionally on the Danube itself by boat. My father was the official doctor for the refugees.

We mostly lived in wagons designed to transport cattle. Each family had a corner, huddled amongst their bundles of belongings. That was home all through the autumn and winter of 1944. Whenever the train stopped, they went to look for food, buying whatever was available from local people. Dried beans and peas were the biggest treasure, worth paying for with gold.

On one stormy night on the boat at Mosonnmagyaróvár, they heard sounds of some wild splashing in the water. They pulled out a confused, drowning diver, tangled amongst the mooring ropes. He was a tall, blond and touchingly young German soldier, hardly older than eighteen, dressed in a wetsuit.

My father attended to him. Like a dripping water-ghost he spluttered, recovered and disappeared into the turbulent murky waters. He didn't say anything and my parents knew better than to ask him. They assumed that he had been sent on an underwater reconnaissance mission, alone, at night with only a feeble torch for company. They hoped he would survive; he must have been someone's much loved son.

The situation of the displaced trainload of Hungarians had changed as we were taken from Hungary to Austria and on to Germany. We were now captive. Near Munich in the middle of a forest we stopped moving and were placed in a refugee camp, a 'Lager'. To begin with there was even some food. How we lived there, what the daily routine was I have no idea.

I seem to recall from stories that the families rigged up sheets to provide some kind of privacy. They all shared the one stove to cook on. I heard that the Lager huts were made of layers of wood providing wonderful insulation; I imagine it must have been some kind of plywood. Family stories never dwelt on our existence there; it was too painful a subject. I think my parents must have been very frightened. But Hitler's Germany was close to collapse by then, and in the general chaos the small Hungarian group somehow escaped notice.

They found that wild sorrel or nettle soup is very nourishing, so is fruit from neglected orchards. By that time, they all wore whatever was most durable. My father sported walking boots, the trousers of a black, finely-striped morning suit and a hunting jacket. From a frayed, worn out heavy winter coat my mum magicked a pinafore dress for herself and a tiny little waistcoat body-warmer for me.

I look at today's cute little garments, the white, fluffy, bunny-rabbit-bespeckled baby rompers, and it breaks my heart whenever I think of my little top.

In hope and despair my mum embroidered that scrap of a dark grey, itchy piece of woollen cloth with red and white daisies for her little daughter: me.

I am a year and a half old, in the refugee camp June, 1945. In the background is the wooden construction that was home.

Me again, at the same time. I can't imagine who took these pictures, there are just four of them and they are only 2x2 cm.

The Pastor's Armchair –
My Grandmother's Story

1944

I am old. I am no use anymore, I can barely walk. So I sit. In this familiar old chair I sit but my dreams and thoughts roam the world, my world. How it used to be... I think of old things and watch the world go by. Thoughts of people around me now and of those long gone, weave in and out of my mind, like colourful threads.

My dear husband used to sit in this chair. Of course in those days we lived in the manse and the armchair was always in his study. He was such a learned man, tall and stern, the good Pastor Gyüre. I can see him now in his study, wearing the black, unadorned Calvinist gown with an equally sober black suit beneath. He sat there, hours on end, in the bluish haze of his pipe smoke, surrounded by his books, writing his sermons, seeing people. Though not much given to gaiety, he was always organising something. He cared for the neediest most, for the families who live at the end of the village in their ramshackle huts. Most of all he wanted their children to be educated. How proud he was when he managed to establish the first lending library in the diocese! His life was the life of the village. People knew that. Everyone is a Calvinist here. No papists. It is a poor parish, no one has much but we have self-respect. Happy days.

He was such a good man, a good husband too, a bit severe, perhaps, but he let me manage the whole household and even bought me my beautiful piano when I wanted to play.

I kept the best kitchen in the neighbourhood. Everyone said so. It's not easy making a good brioche or the lightest of fatless sponge cakes, but I was always accurate and careful. I knew how to make the most complicated recipes. On name days and birthdays we would invite the village teacher, the public notary and their wives, the occasional visiting pastor and, of course, the gauche curates. People of our standing.

Villagers used to give him their money for safekeeping before they went to the front when the Great War came. Yes, honour and truth, that is what he preached and that is how he lived, a blameless Christian life. But where did it get us? The state asked for a war loan from all upstanding Hungarians and Pastor Gyüre, forever a patriot, felt that if the state asks, we must give. He 'loaned' the state everything we had. At the end of the war he could return all the parishioners' money, but we were left penniless. Is there any justice in this world?

And then he was no more. The Lord saw fit to take him away. Not long after the Great War, he had a heart attack and I was left alone, all alone. My dear good husband, I am sitting in your chair. My fingers stroke the smooth, worn wooden arms, searching for your touch. I miss you, and all I can do is to touch what you once touched.

How did I get so old?

It is barely May, May 1944. We are nearly halfway through this new century. Hard to believe it. I am scared.

Rozi brought the chair out for me. It's a good spot, by the kitchen door. So peaceful. Sheltered. The sun on my face, the scent of the lily of the valley mingling with fresh earth; new life everywhere. A few lazy clouds drift across the endless blue sky. It reminds me of the 'floating islands' we used to make, and the children loved it. Poached, sweet, whipped egg whites on the 'lake' of runny yellow custard. Mind, you do need a whole vanilla pod.

I haven't seen a vanilla pod for years... The Jewish travelling salesman used to bring it to the village. Where is he now? Disappeared.

My two broody hens scratch and cluck contentedly around the trunks of the apple trees, guarding their chicks. I'll have twenty-four young ones, should be enough to see us through.

Rozi is very good to me. Willing. She is widowed

too and lives in the village. My boys pay her wages. I couldn't afford it on my own.

I can keep an eye on everything from here, that's why I like it here. I can see the street, the garden with Ilma and the baby, as Rozi is cooking dinner behind me. Not much today, tomato soup from last year's bottled tomatoes and egg gnocchi with young lettuce from the garden. Well, what can we do? In a few weeks we'll have spring chicken but until then we just have to manage on what's left in the pantry.

Oh, what meals we had when I was a girl, especially when we had visitors, or a big name day. I was one of nine children, there was always something happening, something to celebrate with a good meal. On the white damask tablecloth we would start with a steaming beef soup, clear, rich, pale yellow with those tiny pools of fat, each a miniature golden sun swimming on top.

In a flat dish beside the tureen sat the whitish trembling marrow from the shinbone with wafer thin toast to spread it on. Next we would have the boiled beef with vegetables from the soup, and then came a magnificent stuffed roasted capon, parsley potatoes and all manner of pickled vegetables.

Cakes would be brought in afterward: walnut, hazelnut, chocolate, thickly layered with butter cream and then fruit compotes: sour cherry, apricot, peach. We always had a glass or two of local wine too. Shall I tell you the secret of a good beef soup? You must cook it very, very slowly and for a long time. It should hardly bubble. And don't forget to seal the ends of the marrow bones well with salt, otherwise the marrow will seep out and make the soup cloudy.

Oh, but it's gone, all gone.

The schoolteacher's wife has just walked past and she waved. Where is she going? She should be home, at half past eleven, getting the meal ready for her husband. He was lucky, he hasn't been called up.

Ilma and the baby in the garden! That girl is reading again, the baby asleep in the basket beside her. They are both called Ilma. Dezső wanted it like this, they said, but they could have called her after me... Never mind. Still, my daughter-in-law and my granddaughter here in my garden!

How strange, I never thought it would happen.

Laci, my elder boy, at forty-five, is still not married and Dezső was forty-two when he finally decided.

Why is she still reading? How quiet that girl is. Nice enough when you talk to her, good family, well brought up. With her looks, that thick dark, dark hair, those big brown eyes, you would have thought there was more life in her. My hair never was that dark, it was thin and straight too but I could joke and tease at her age. I wasn't fat then of course. What a figure I had!

I wonder if the baby is awake yet. Can't hear a thing. Ilma is still reading. How can she sit for so long? She could be baking! My book is full of recipes I have collected over the years and I've hardly tried any of them. Who would I have made cakes for? I have been alone for almost twenty years now, all alone, waiting for a time when I will have life around me again, grandchildren, large family, big dinners, and lots of cakes, laughter, and music. Well, it did not turn out like that. The boys grew up and were gone, living their own lives, hardly a thought for me. And now Ilma, this silent girl, is here and she doesn't really want to bake.

Is that the postman I saw just now going by? It must be another telegram for someone in the village. I wonder who it is. So much death. How many now, in the village? Awful, awful. So much sadness.

Oh dear God, help my boys! Let them be safe! They will be, surely, surely! If God is with us, who can be against us? Laci is an army judge, they won't send him to the front and Dezső as a doctor was needed in the hospital in Ungvár, so mercifully he wasn't called up, but the Eastern front is getting so close. The Russians are near.

There are some awful rumours in the village, the same stories go round and round, everyone adds to the stories and they become ever more frightening. No one knows what to believe... They say that the Russians are all beasts, six foot tall, blond, cruel beasts. They rape women, they loot, they eat horses and some of them are not even Russians, they come from somewhere far, far east and have slanting eyes with a face like a dog. I will not think these dreadful thoughts...Oh Father, deliver us from evil.

Are the Germans any better though? We are

allies; of course they won't harm us. Our Father, who art in Heaven.

Baby is waking up. Not a pretty child but good tempered. My own little girl was just a bit older when... When.

It was Christmas Eve and Lenke, my little daughter, was reaching with her chubby little arm for the shining bell on the tree. She was laughing as the two boys played hide and seek with her, ringing the little bell. We were so happy. My dear husband and I laughed at their high spirits. Little Lenke was a bit hot but she only had a little rash. The next morning we found her dead.

A lot of children died that year.

Did you know that Lenke means little linen flower? Her eyes were such a clear light blue, just like mine.

I don't know how to look at Ilma's daughter. It hurts so much. She too has blue eyes, my eyes. I would like to hold her but Ilma is possessive and to be honest I am a little afraid too, it's a long time since I held a baby. What will become of her? Poor little mite, to be born in these dreadful, uncertain times. The washing is on the line. It's blowing nicely. Such a lovely breezy day. All those nappies, like flags waving, announcing to the world that we HAVE A BABY in the house. Wonderful.

Dezső said he would come soon. Then we might go. Go where? Wherever we are safe he said.

Lead us, Lord.

Thy will be done.

The pastor's widow, Grandmother Lenke and myself, early 1944

There I am, all alone in the old chair, 1944

34

Tiszaderzs Calvinist Church.

Pastor and Mrs Gyüre in the centre, my father between his
father's knees, his sister next to her mother, and big brother
László on the left. The others are my grandmother's brothers,
sisters and their families. 1905

Pastor Gyüre, 1920

Recipe of my Grandmother's Magnificent Beef Soup with Marrowbone

The soup should be hot, crystal clear, pale yellowish brown, with just a small amount of golden fat on top. The dumplings are a richer yellow, very light and uniform in shape.

Ingredients:
800g boiling beef, preferably with some fat
4-6 largish beef shin bones, with marrow inside
1 large brown onion
4-5 large carrots
3-4 Hamburg parsley roots
1 small celeriac
1 young kohlrabi
1 bunch of parsley
2-3 cloves of garlic
Segment of the hard core of drumhead cabbage or one large leaf
1 small hot pepper
Whole peppercorns
Pinch of saffron
Salt

Method:

1. Wash the meat and bones, salt the open marrow ends of the bones.
2. In a large saucepan boil slowly for about an hour, taking off the scum as it rises.
3. Leaving the brown skin on the onion, add the vegetables apart from carrots to the soup.
4. Cook very slowly, so that it hardly bubbles for at least another hour.
5. Now add the carrots, which should be in longish chunks.
6. Cook slowly for another half an hour.
7. Sieve the hot soup into a serving dish, offer semolina dumplings (see following page) in a separate dish.
8. Knock marrow out of the bones into a smaller bowl, with a spoonful of hot soup.
9. Serve the soup with semolina dumplings, and the hot marrow with salt and thin toast immediately.
10. Place the meat and carrots on a serving plate and keep warm. Discard the unwanted vegetables.
11. Serve this after the soup, as a second course.

Semolina Dumplings

Ingredients:
2 eggs
6 tablespoons semolina
Pinch each of salt and bicarbonate of soda

Method:
1. Beat the eggs until frothy.
2. Add the salt and bicarbonate of soda.
3. Slowly add the semolina, mixing until smooth – it should still be fairly liquid.
4. Rest in a cool place for 30 minutes – the dough will become firmer.
5. Bring a large saucepan of salty water to a gentle boil.
6. With two dessert spoons, shape 'torpedoes' and gently lower them into the simmering water.
7. Cook the dumplings for 15 minutes – they will rise to the top. Do not stir.
8. Ladle some of the hot soup into another dish, place the dumplings in the liquid, cover and leave to absorb the taste for 20 mins.
9. Serve with the soup.

Extract from my Mother's Letter to my Father

1 Sept 1944

My dear darling Dezső,

It is such a terrible torture that I have no news of you at all. I walk to the post office every single evening, so that I don't have to wait till the morning delivery but there is never anything from you.

Your mother is convinced that you are in trouble but you don't want to alarm us. My dear, there is nothing wrong, is there? And if there was, you wouldn't hide it from me surely? May God help you and preserve you!

I got several cards and a letter from my mother after the two days bombing in Budapest, she and Alice are all right. But I don't know when or where the bombs fell, and I am too afraid to enquire.

I am so worried for all of you; the situation seems so bad, God alone can help us now.

My darling, if only I could see your writing, I

would be a bit calmer. You are so terribly far away from me and I would so much like to be reassured by your words.

God will, perhaps, be merciful to us.

I only smile when I look at the little girl, she is so sweet. She likes tomato juice with saccharine.

If you can't send a note from Ungvár, could you not go to the next town and send at least a telegram from there?

Postscript

1949 – The Present

In 1949 when my grandmother died, Rákosi's rabid communist regime declared her, the Calvinist minister's widow whose main interest in life was her family and cooking, an 'enemy of the people' and her belongings were considered fair game.

The house itself was commandeered by the Hungarian State Post Office, though my father still owned the building and had to pay for all the upkeep. It was eventually released in 1966. He sold it and divided the proceeds in two, for my sister and myself.

I was now married and living in England. When my mother and father came in 1968 to visit me, they naturally travelled by train, across Europe. A plane would have been unthinkable, way beyond our means.

They took the Wiener Walzer from Budapest to Vienna, the Balt-Orient Express from Vienna to Ostend, than a ferry to Dover and train again from

Dover to Victoria, just as I did a few years before when I came to Britain. I was waiting for them there, in the busy station, l was pleased, excited. At last there they were. I saw them from a distance, standing on the platform: a little, obviously Eastern European couple, looking as forlorn and miserable as a wet weekend in August.

I was bewildered. It was not the joyous reunion I was expecting. They had to tell me there and then, standing on the platform: They had brought my share in cash in an envelope, carefully buttoned in the inside pocket of my father's jacket. By the time they docked in Dover the envelope had been stolen.

Frankly, I was relieved that that was all it was. Don't say it! Large amount of cash, in an envelope, in a jacket pocket? But they did want to give it to us with a flourish; they knew that David and I were living none too lavishly, on David's research-student grant. My grandmother's much-loved beautiful, satinwood grand piano had been claimed by the local pub, for the entertainment of the rougher elements of the local agrarian proletariat. It never recovered from having beer poured into it.

However, some bits of furniture, two kitchen chairs, the much-loved and used pastor's armchair and some remains of her trousseau, like hand-woven linen tablecloths, napkins and tea towels, were rescued for the family by friends in the village.

I inherited the shape of her blue eyes, my sister her fierce loyalty and incredible attention to detail.

43

My Sister and that Tablecloth

1945

Is it possible to return with more than you left with from a harrowing exile, although emaciated, hungry and with all valuables exchanged for food? Yes, in our case! Because, amidst all the confusion, the bombings, Germany's capitulation, hardship and hunger, my mother got pregnant, right there, in the 'Lager' in Germany.

My dear, clever, caring doctor father deemed it wise to have the new baby in a hospital. He would think that; he was a hospital doctor himself, he trusted the system. That is all well and fine, except the hospital was rather a long way off from the plywood huts in the woods, where the Hungarian refugees were housed.

When the birth seemed imminent he therefore hired a horse and cart from a farmer to take her. It must have been a beautiful trip, ripe, beautiful autumn, early September in the woods. However, all that splendour was lost on my mother. No birdsong for her and no rustling leaves, for the roads were only dirt tracks, the cart had no springs and she was in the last stages of labour.

They simply had to stop. Luckily, they were just passing a convent. Urgent thumping on the heavy, firmly shut wooden doors eventually produced a cautious nun, peeping out through a tiny slit. It took some time before she understood why their peace had been so rudely shattered.

Meanwhile my poor mother was standing there, in front of the wooden door, in agony. At last, they were let in to the entrance hall, where my mother stood, still in agony. The nuns belonged to a contemplative order. No doubt they were very experienced in spiritual matters but the imminent birth of a real life baby threw them into utter confusion. Like a flock of agitated, large crows they flew here and flew there all over the convent, their habits fluttering, leaving my panting mother still just standing. Eventually a quick-thinking nun fetched a goodly sized enamel hand basin and pushed it underneath her, and there, squatting on the floor in the entrance hall of a convent, into a metal bowl my lovely sister Zsuzsi, (Susannah) was born.

My father had his wish though, soon after the birth the same horse and cart transported the new-born and her mother to the nearest hospital in the townlet of Griesbach.

When I said my lovely sister Zsuzsi, I have

45

jumped ahead of time somewhat because she was a wizened little thing at first. How could she have been any other way? And our mother had no milk to feed her. Again, how could it have been any other way?

To their immense relief they found a woman who had that priceless commodity, breast milk, to spare. But baby Zsuzsi failed to thrive. Her initial lusty cry turned into just a mournful meowing of a Siamese kitten. How could she know that her helpless mother sobbed beside her? Eventually, they had realised that they paid a very high price for a lot of water and very little milk. I am still angry with that unknown woman, who for sheer greed watered down the breast milk and put my sister's life in jeopardy.

Somehow, though, we all survived.

When the Americans took over the refugee camp in Germany in 1945, we were given a choice: Would you wish to go to America – land of freedom and plenty – or would you like to go back to Hungary?

Home, home to Hungary, was the only choice for them, wondering, praying and hoping that the rest of our family were still alive. By now it was early summer 1946 and their journey began.

The ancient steam engine puffed, coughed a bit and with hiccup-like whistles ground to a halt at a small, dilapidated station. As it stood motionless, tranquillity reigned once again amongst the gentle hills of western Hungary.

'Not again!' grumbled the passengers and would have looked out of the window, if they had any. But they were travelling in cattle wagons, so they had to slide a heavy door, just to ascertain where they might be this time. They were almost too weary to bother. For that particular group this train journey was not the first one. For them it meant that the war was over and they could come home.

It was very different from their first train journey, back in 1944, when as displaced citizens they were evacuated by train to the very heartland of trouble, to a refugee camp in Germany. The trainload, some forty Hungarians, was part of the repatriation scheme. There, amongst them was our little family: my mother, father, his mother, my baby sister and myself, a toddler. We'd lived in these wagons for weeks now, each family occupying a corner, here they slept, cooked on rudimentary camping stoves, if there was anything to cook, and washed as well as they could. The train had started from near Munich, passing through the length of Austria and had now finally crossed the Hungarian border.

There was not a lot to see: a ticket office, some low buildings, a few hens scratching near the rails, a water crane for the engine, and the solitary stationmaster in attendance. Word went round that it would take two hours to refuel. Good news that there was fuel, but the passengers were exhausted and hungry.

Nine months after the end of the Second World

War, the devastating effects of the six years' bitter fighting were still visible all over Europe. Wherever the war had touched, there were families torn apart, towns in ruins, derelict factories, and damaged railway lines, blown up bridges, food shortages and disease. People, whichever side they were originally from, suffered. They tried to come to terms with the losses, to rebuild and return to normality.

So it was with the Hungarians too. Since April 1945, Hungary was a Russian-occupied country, and the administration was in chaos, the agriculture in ruins. At least no one was shooting around us anymore; this was a distinct advantage but there was even less food. My mother was given an onion once, an occasion so memorable that it stayed with her all her life. She ate it eagerly, raw as it was, crisp and crunchy, and it tasted better than any apple she remembered.

How on earth my parents managed in that cattle wagon to look after and feed a toddler, a baby sister, who had continuous diarrhoea, and my feeble grandmother, I cannot even begin to imagine. I must have been constantly warned of the dangers because I harboured a mythical fear well into adulthood of railway lines, bumpers on wagons, and those heavy sliding doors.

Once we crossed the Danube, my grandmother, my father's mother, parted from our little party to return to her village, Tiszaderzs. As nothing was known of the whereabouts of her elder son, László, the soldier, she was anxious to return home and wait. She felt that if he were still alive, surely, that was where he would look for her.

The train kept stopping erratically and the progress was painfully slow, but this time they were joyously going HOME, to Szeged, to my mother's family. And, after an unexpected detour to the small town of Kiskunhalas, on a fine, early summer morning in 1946, we arrived in Szeged.

I wasn't yet three, but I do have some memory of the event. I vaguely recall the rattle-bump, rattle-bump of the porter's hand-pulled cart on the cobblestones during the long walk from the station, me proudly sitting on top of the bundles. My grandmother's living room, however, is a very clear memory. I saw the floor, the polished, herringbone pattern of the parquet and could not make any visual sense of it, it felt as if we were shifting or tilting. I was only used to small, dark, enclosed spaces like a cattle wagon and I yelled in fright.

Little Zsuzsi bawled in enthusiastic unison.

Still, even though noisy, the newest family member was admired. And now my mother cried, my grandmother cried, my two aunts cried, even the two sons-in-law joined in with a manly sniffle or two, but I was the only one who was afraid of the parquet. The relief that they were all alive and together must have been overwhelming.

Zsuzsi would not stop crying. 'This child is hungry,' the grownups realised. Quickly they cooked some semolina pudding, that's all they had, and Zsuzsi was fed. After that everyone realised that they too were hungry. So there was semolina pudding all round, the most festive, celebratory meal, equal to any fatted calf, anyone could ever have.

Zsuzsi grew, bandy-legged, to begin with, the legacy of lack of vitamins, but cuddly, with the sweetest of smiles. She toddled behind me.

She wasn't a child for lily-livered parents though. Zsuzsi had a will and she knew what she did not want. Afternoon sleep? NO, said Zsuzsi, standing on top of her toy box on her chubby little O-shaped legs, clinging to the bars of her playpen, bringing the house down with her crying. 'Do your homework' – much later. 'NO, don't want to.' 'Time to get up to go to school!' 'No, no, no!'

Whereas I always tried to be compliant, Zsuzsi was confrontational and stubbornly believed that what she wanted was right for herself. I suppose her early starvation, which she experienced as abandonment, made her feel that she had to fight for her very existence. It shaped her strong will; which ultimately served her well throughout her life.

We are physically alike, my sister and I, tall, blonde, blue eyed but very different in interests. On Sunday afternoons, two daughters dressed alike – which we hated equally – the family would go for gentle walks, usually Zsuzsi with my mother, me with my father. I would chat with my dad about whatever occurred to me, but Zsuzsi always inquired after something concrete, like how paper was made or what tools cavemen had. I remember thinking how dull all that was. Of course she was encouraged in her quest for knowledge; though her famous scientific experiment did not go down all that well. Aged six or seven, she chopped off part of the fringe of a beautifully embroidered tablecloth, just to see if it was like human hair and would grow again. It did not, at least not to this day.

I have a confession to make. I promised at the beginning of my stories that I would take you round my Budapest flat and tell you about each of the items there which have family history connected to them. I couldn't show you this particular tablecloth though. I have many others, equally antique, but this one, so beautiful, so fresh with its cross-stitched stylised red roses, my sister claimed. We agreed that she is the rightful custodian.

I loved drawing and painting. In fact it occupied much of my thoughts, observing colours and shapes, trying to reproduce them, and not succeeding, or creating rhythmic patterns – very, very satisfying.

Zsuzsi did none of that. Only once was she stirred to create something magnificent. The source of her inspiration was the neighbour's freshly whitewashed, immaculate wall. She drew a rather large tulip there, with the sap of some green leaves. I thought her mural was well placed and effective; sadly the owners of the wall were not artistic enough to appreciate it. They were angry, our parents apologetic, Zsuzsi disappointed. She had no idea that she had done anything wrong.

That was the end of her artistic endeavour. Instead she became a doctor, a very good one, knowledgeable and caring, like our father.

Our mother, a couple of months before my sister was born in the refugee camp, summer 1945.

Bowlegged Zsuzsi, one year old (result of all the hardship), 1946.

With our mother in Szeged, at our grandmother's apartment. Zsuzsi is in Mother's arms, 1946.

We are growing up, 1948.

Portrait of Zsuzsi, 1947.

Zsuzsi is getting married to Tamás, 1968.

Zsuzsi, the young doctor, with her husband, mother and aunt,
Alice.

Gabi and Gyuri, Zsuzsi's children, with their Gyüre
grandparents, 1975.

Table with Stalin's Portrait

1947

So we were safely accommodated, and settled, for a while at least, with my maternal grandmother, Ida, in Szeged. She had all her three daughters, Ilma, Anci and Alice under her roof. The two married daughters' husbands, my father and Anci's husband Miklós were here too and us, the children. It must have been pretty tight accommodation but nobody minded.

Always quietly spoken, only amongst the closest family circle and trusted friends, the words 'Before the war...' and 'When the Russians came in...' popped up again and again in grown-up conversations. This assumed a forbidden and almost mythical significance for us children, for we were not meant to overhear such talk. A never-never land of ancient times, six or even ten years ago, a time immeasurable when you are not quite five yourself and your sister is just three. Not even very interesting.

From our perspective, life was good. It followed a reliable, set pattern, loving, quiet, ordered and clean. Breakfast of milk with bread and jam for the children, chicory coffee for the grownups. Cooked lunch was always based on vegetables, with fruit to follow, yoghurt and bread or cottage cheese in the evening and, possibly, the once-a-week miracle of meat on Sundays.

Of course it was not like this 'before the war'. We didn't miss it though, and did not even quite believe in those golden times. And there was proof that we should not. My mother came home from shopping one day, proudly waving a tiny brown paper bag and said, 'I got you something, something we used to have before the war.'

Out came on to a saucer, some little brown shrivelled things: 'Five for you and five for your sister.' We tried these squashed-fly-looking things but were not impressed, yet we could see that they were very special for her. 'They are called raisins,' she said, almost in tears.

Oh, but we had an orange once! Now that was a vision of unimaginable beauty, a perfect globe of glowing colour, a messenger of lands and people so far off, from a place called Italy, where none of us could ever hope to get to. The Orange was first duly admired, placed on a large plate in the living room and looked at from every angle. I liked the skin, not smooth like an apple, much more like real skin but still shiny somehow. My mother started to peel it –

we watched in awe. Two incisions, carefully, carefully so that the orange peel came away in four petals, displaying a white globe, as if the fruit was wearing a brushed cotton vest, just like the ones we wore in winter.

I tasted the white bit. It was not very good, still I chewed it. And then came the real excitement. It was in segments, each bit parcelled up neatly, just right for sharing. A wonderful burst of flavour in your mouth when you ate it, an unforgettable sensation. I have never again had such a wonderful orange but am still looking for one.

'Of course, before the war,' said my father wistfully, 'when I travelled all over Italy, I ate lots of these and,' he added with a certain shy pride, 'in Verona, a very beautiful woman playfully threw me an orange from her carriage as I walked past.'

My mother changed the subject and sliced up the orange peel in minute shreds, to be stored in sugar, '...because it will make cakes taste wonderful,' she said.

The living room in my grandmother's first floor apartment, scene of The Orange's final and glittering performance, was furnished with rather lovely antiques, mainly from the first half of the 19th century, in the Biedermeier style. They were all old, family pieces. All clean, restrained, curving lines and nothing ostentatious, like a swan settee, some low, round-backed armchairs, a few small tables, and a chest of drawers with delicate inlay, overall giving the illusion of blond, sunny peace, as the summer light filtered through the half-drawn wooden blinds.

I loved watching as the sun picked out the dancing particles of dust in the air and on the parquet floor, the antique Persian rugs, like contented cats, glowed in saturated, joyous colours. This room was definitely grown-up and visitor territory and, obviously, fitting for The Orange.

It is a miracle that in 1947 all this furniture from 'before the war' was still there. When the Russian army occupied Szeged, mercifully there was no fighting, although the locals received a very clear message of who was in charge and who had lost the war.

Looting was the order of the day; Russian soldiers were allowed to take anything they wanted from anyone. All they needed was to knock on a door, walk in and grab what took their fancy. They seemed to have a liking for wristwatches, often wearing six to eight on each arm. Strangely, this multiple watch-wearing habit gave the Hungarians some kind of moral superiority; they could at least laugh at the 'barbarians'.

My grandmother also had a visit, her lovely apartment was ransacked. What happened next? My grandmother loved to tell the story later, and we loved to hear it.

'A couple of days after the robbery, Alice and I were walking in town and saw a Russian army lorry, open at the back, packed to the brim with furniture.

We looked in, and Alice said, "Mum, that is our table, just there!"

"'It can't be.'"

"'But it is, that's our table!'"

'So we looked around, and there was not a Russian soldier in sight. Alice jumped up on the lorry, handed down the table, and the two of us walked calmly away, holding two legs each, as if this was the most natural thing in the world.' Nobody stopped them.

The image of our gentle grandmother, who always wore black, mourning her husband's death in 1928, who could not say a harsh word to anyone even if she tried, and timid Alice, together thieving from a Russian army lorry delighted us. As I said, we wanted to hear the story again and again.

'Only when we got home did we see that some artistic Russian had scratched a very recognisable portrait of Stalin into the fine veneer.'

I wonder if my readers can hear the complexity of that one sentence and the irony? Artistic and Russian just did not fit together in that story. It was felt that to deliberately scratch an elegant antique piece was tantamount to sacrilege, only a barbarian would do it. And to scratch a portrait of Stalin, the most feared, loathed despot of our age added insult to injury. It was as if some ghastly voodoo devil appeared in our cosy circle. But there was pity as well – that poor Russian soldier – what a false god he was worshipping! And at the end of it all, one had to admit, it was a good portrait.

'Look,' said my grandmother years later, pulling aside the gossamer–fine white lace cloth. 'Here it is.' And there it was.

The other table lost and found was small, round-topped, and of ebony wood. For its leg it had a beautifully carved 'savage', in a grass skirt, picked out in gold leaf. After it was taken, it was spotted by the door of a dubious manicure salon for 'ladies who accompanied' the Russian army. My plucky aunt nicked that one back too and it is now with my cousin Ida.

When my grandmother died, my mother inherited the table, as well as the round-back, low armchairs. And after her death, I am now their custodian. My mother had Stalin's portrait erased. And this is why on the Biedermeier table, right in the middle, among the scratches of 200 years there is a pristine patch. But if you look very carefully, in the slanting sunlight, you can just see the remnants of some Cyrillic writing. I am so glad that it is still there.

'Uncle' Lajos and his wife, 1950s. They were also Transylvanian and he was my grandfather's caretaker in the 1920s. After the Russians looted Grandmother's apartment, they took her and Alice in and fed them for months.

Zsuzsi and myself with our father, 1946, on the inner balcony in front of my grandmother's door. This photo, more than any other, seems to encapsulate the mood and conditions immediately after the war. Look at our clothes, the shoes and the homemade rabbit toy I am holding. The walls bear the signs of recent stray bullets, but look at the love which surrounds us; and we feel secure and pretty, with ribbons in our hair.

Horsehair Mattresses

1948

I wonder if anyone these days even knows what a horsehair mattress is.

They are small. Three of them put together make a single bed, six a comfortable double. They are light to carry, firm, with just enough 'give' to ensure a good night's sleep, and a double layer is sheer heaven. I have twelve of them. Nowadays, they are stored in airtight bags and only come out if I have extra overnight visitors.

In my mother's time the grandchildren used to sleep on them on the floor, like on a futon.

The horses, whose long manes and tail hair were so capably stitched together, have long galloped their last. My mattresses are about 100 years old, expertly cleaned and re-covered many, many times.

Back in 1948 the handwritten notice:

Clean, good quality household items for sale. Enquire 3rd floor, Appt. 14

caused quite a stir in the elegant Szeged tenement

block where we stayed with my grandmother. The L-shaped three-storey building overlooked a pleasant courtyard with a continuous, wrought iron, internal balcony. All front doors, all kitchen windows opened from there, while the high-ceilinged, huge-windowed living rooms faced the quiet street.

Perfect circumstances for neighbours to exchange pleasantries or stick their noses into other peoples' business.

Have you heard my dear? They are selling everything!

What, EVERYTHING?

I wonder what they have?

A nice family...

Keep themselves to themselves though.

They were always very house proud.

Yes, the stuff will certainly be very clean.

I could do with some jam jars.

And we really need some chairs.

And the procession to the third floor began, the necessary decorum mingled with curiosity, need, an eye for a bargain, and plain greed; as it would do anywhere.

Many families, including ours, had lost everything in the war, not a piece of furniture was left. My mother bought some horsehair mattresses. Now, at last, we had our own beds.

The news that the Meyerhofs were emigrating

spread like wildfire through the building. They were selling everything because they were leaving to go to Israel. This was THE topic of conversation, guardedly on the balconies, but more freely in the safety behind locked doors.

Israel, such a newly formed state, so uncertain a future. What will await them there? How brave they are to risk everything for an idea! – was the general consensus. People tended to worry about what lay ahead of the Meyerhof family, with little or no understanding of what lay behind them.

This contemporary lack of understanding is almost impossible to believe now. From the 8,700 Jews in Szeged 6,600 were deported and only 1,500 returned.

So how could people not have been aware?

I have only felt myself in mortal danger once in my life. I was returning from Belfast on what was meant to be a half-hour evening flight to Manchester. A fierce storm developed during the flight and as our little plane was violently tossed, the stewardesses were shuffling about on their knees handing out sick-bags. We lurched towards the Manchester runway, the wheels were lowered, we were nearly there, nearly landed, but the pilot did not dare risk touchdown and drunkenly our plane took off again towards the only open airport, Nottingham.

Elated to feel solid ground beneath our feet, we gratefully left the plane and waited for instructions in the terminal, chatting to fellow passengers. And waited. And waited. Somehow there did not seem to be any ground staff anywhere, no one in authority, though we searched for them. The storm was still raging outside and in the apocalyptic gloom more plane-loads arrived, more and more disturbed people were milling around. It dawned on us gradually that nothing was going to happen, no instructions, no onward help.

The mood changed. The pleasant businessman I had talked to previously suddenly became hostile, jealously guarding his scheme for his journey home. Rumour had it that there were buses outside. Cue a tremendous surge of jostling people, finding the long-distance buses. I asked the driver of the Manchester bus if I could get on. 'Sure love,' was the answer, but a man with clipboard appeared and got me off the bus, saying 'only for pre-booked passengers.' Then the news spread: All motorways were now closed, no buses were going anywhere, but the trains were still running.

We besieged the local buses and, still buffeted by wind, but fortunately not up in the air any more, arrived to a chaotic, heaving station, only to find all trains cancelled.

The only person I knew in Nottingham was an ex-colleague of my husband's from the seventies. Some frantic phone calls located him and I begged for a bed for the night. Next morning, as he had business to attend to in Manchester, he drove me home, in the brilliant sunshine.

What shocked me, after the serious consideration that we might crash, was how very thin our layer of civilisation really is. How at the beginning we all trusted the authorities and waited for instructions, and when it was not forthcoming, what bitter competitors we all became. We all wanted to get home, to safety, but if there were room for only a certain number; we wanted to be amongst these. We only watched other people to see if they had a better solution than us, not because we were in any way compassionate or caring. And I honestly don't know what happened to any of my fellow passengers. All this was in 2008, in prosperous, peacetime Britain.

Imagine the same group psychology, magnified a million times. Bombing was real, death and destruction everyday occurrences, the Hungarian army was destroyed, leaving the government impotent against the pincer attack of Nazis from the West and Russians from the East.

Like a disturbed ants' nest, everyone was running somewhere, cumbersomely carting bundles of what was precious to them; be it children, eiderdowns, silver, a medical diploma or dried beans. Ordinary families packed up their belongings, locked up their apartments and fled.

In this mad scramble it was an everyday occurrence that neighbours disappeared without saying goodbye. Some calculated that somewhere, far away from the centre, tiny villages would be safe. Others thought that big towns with many inhabitants would be a better bet. To get away from the Eastern front, my parents boarded a refugee train just before the 1944 Nazi invasion of Hungary. We are not Jewish; it is a sad historical fact that I can even prove this because in the forties everyone had to verify their ethnic and religious origins, but my parents felt that the safest place would be keeping ahead of the conflict.

The other part of my family, my grandmother, her married daughter with her husband and small child, and other daughter felt that Budapest, right next to the Castle, would be the safest place to be.

Hitler invaded Hungary in March 1944. Within three months Hungary was Judenfrei. Those who could, hid, or left the country using forged documents, but still, 450,000 Hungarian Jews lost their lives. What happened and how it happened in its full unspeakable, unthinkable horror only gradually became common knowledge. Partly because the Stalinist regime was reluctant to touch the topic since they were similarly guilty. Many Jewish families were still searching, even hoping. Others were too traumatised or grieving.

It was only in the early sixties that I myself understood this tragedy.

Pretty, thirty something Mrs Polák, our Hungarian teacher, talked about the Jewish poet Radnóti who had died in 1944. His last slim volume, written during a forced march, was found in his pocket in the mass grave.

Quietly, serenely, our teacher talked about her own lost family and the concentration camps. She wasn't crying, she did not even raise her voice. Awestruck, we listened. She told us because we needed to know and with incredible bravery and generosity allowed us to grieve with her. It was a life-changing experience.

Let me erect an imaginary statue here to her: A slim young woman, a lucky Anne Frank, sitting on top of a school bench, legs neatly tucked under, bending forward so that she is close to her pupils, teaching us how to be human.

How could it happen in Hungary? Who is guilty of the mass murder of our fellow Hungarians? Are our parents culpable? Or can we just conveniently say, 'The Nazis,' not us, someone else? These questions have haunted Hungarian consciences ever since.

Anti-Semitism has been long present in Hungary, as indeed in many other European countries. Sophisticated lateral thinking, wit, talent, business acumen, added to a strong group cohesion felt like a threat in a society where inherited title was deemed to be enough to claim privileges. Yet until the end of the First World War, the ruling upper middle class only practised a polite 'salon anti-Semitism', accepting Jewish people, but somehow tactfully 'not noticing' that they were Jewish, as if it were some kind of a physical disfigurement.

The defeat in 1918 was swiftly followed by a

bloody uprising, the 'Commune' (led by the Jewish International communist Béla Kun). The national reaction to the disastrous loss of Hungarian territories was a search for a scapegoat. Somehow, the Jews were blamed.

In 1938, Horthy aligned the country with Germany. In return he was able to reclaim some of the 'lost' territories of Hungary, like Transylvania, Slovakia and the 'low Carpathian'.

Anti-Jewish legislation started in 1938 but was not acted upon. During 1939, all Jewish men of military age were drafted into 'work battalions'. People knew about this. It didn't seem to be too threatening at the time, and the majority of Jews lived safely in Hungary while Hungarians were in charge. Even in Ungvár, this far eastern town of Hungary there were 'work battalion' Jewish doctors in my father's hospital. 'What was it like for them?' I asked as a teenager. 'Good doctors, decent men,' said my father. 'They were treated like anybody else.' That is what he knew at the time.

Nevertheless, the net was laid; and when the Nazis invaded Hungary in 1944 they could act with ghastly speed.

Many of those who were aware did help. Many others pretended not to see for fear of reprisals. And there were those Hungarians who became murderers.

Before the Second World War no one could even begin to imagine mass murder on such a scale. It is different for us now. We know that it CAN happen. Any organised segregation can and might lead to heinous consequences. We can't escape our responsibility.

I don't know how the Meyerhofs managed to survive. I don't know what happened to them after they left for Israel, but I would like to think that they lived in peace and prosperity. It would be rather wonderful though, if some of their descendants found me and I could say to them, 'Look, your great-grandparents slept on this.'

The Unexpected Detour
and the Necklace Which Is No More

1946

I talked about the incident on our homeward journey to Szeged when the steam train had to stop at Kiskunhalas for lack of fuel, only to resume the remaining few hours' journey a day later.

There are some unexpected detours in one's life, which at the time seem irksome but turn out to be the beginning of a series of life-changing events. Stopping at Kiskunhalas was one of these events for us. Nowadays, this unremarkable small town is less than an hour's drive away from Szeged, but back in 1946 it seemed eons away. The dispirited passengers were angry, exhausted, dirty and hungry, and still a day away from home. Still, it could not be helped. My father resignedly did what he always did whenever the train stopped; he went to look for food.

He had no money but had a method. So typical of him. Throughout his life he analysed the circumstances he found himself in and devised a course of action.

His method throughout the journey was to find the local Calvinist minister, or the local doctor or the hospital if there was one. He reckoned they would understand his predicament and might be in the position to help with some food. He was right, they did.

I can see him, the lonely figure walking on the long, featureless road from the station. Battered, faded khaki rucksack on his back, inside it an empty three-tiered aluminium food container. He carried it, just in case, more in good hope than conviction that it might be useful.

He had had a good wash at the station tap before setting off, his hands scrubbed; face clean, straight hair neatly combed away from his intelligent forehead. Asking for help was very difficult for him. He still wore the same pair of trousers of his erstwhile elegant, narrow-striped black morning suit, but so baggy, even the tightly-pulled belt could hardly keep it up, as he now only weighed eight stone.

The same old mountain walking boots still held, although they had not seen any polish for a long, long time, and his fine, monogrammed shirt, crumpled but clean, seemed to have been made for someone much larger. With a wry smile he mused that he must look not unlike Charlie Chaplin, whose films he had loved, in what seemed another life. Nobody batted an eyelid though as he walked on;

people were used to strange fashions in those days.

'Just go straight,' they said, 'turn left after the statue. But it is a good walk from here.'

There he trudged, head slightly bent forward, as if battling an undetectable wind.

'I am not begging!' he argued with himself. As a proud and private man he would much rather give, and preferred to do it unseen. 'This is not begging! I am asking for help. If the situation was reversed, I would give whatever I could.' And with new resolution, head bent against the non-existent wind he walked on. 'I must somehow feed my family!'

Nearing the town centre, he was pleased to see the houses so familiar in this part of the country. He felt at home.

This is obviously a place which knows fierce heat; everything is arranged so that there is welcome shade from the scorching rays of the summer sun. Well-spaced, square or L-shaped bungalows, with high roofs, two or three windows overlooking the street, shaded verandas following the whole inside length of the buildings. The gardens are large, the front has flowers and further back there is room enough for a few vegetables, poultry, even one or two pigs.

The occasional horse and cart of a farmer rattled past, dogs barked half-heartedly as he walked by the high fences, otherwise hardly any sound disturbed the rose-scented peace.

The tree-lined quiet streets became gradually

grander as he progressed, with the houses of well-to-do burghers along with some public buildings. There was the solid block of the mid-19th century Grammar School, the imposing jury building, the ornate, Art Nouveau town hall. Finally, he reached the charming, whitewashed baroque Calvinist church, with its star at the top of the steeple. This sight pleased him and gave him hope. But the parson was not home.

That left the hospital to try. He asked to see the director, whom he learned was Dr László Monszpart.

Dr Monszpart was there, and he listened. He could see beyond this scarecrow of a man, straight out of the cattle wagon, with the honest, open face. My father told him that he was a doctor and that he had graduated at Budapest Medical School, studied paediatrics under Prof Heim there, followed by postgraduate years in Berlin where he gained another specialist qualification in urology.

Dr Monszpart was a deeply Catholic man and most compassionate. He gave us food, whatever he could spare, and told my father to go back to the station and bring his family with him so that we could all have a bath as well!

'When you have all finished, come and see me for a chat,' he said. The director was thorough; they covered a wide range of topics. It came up in conversation that my grandfather had been a Calvinist minister. 'I like the sons of Calvinist ministers,' said Dr Monszpart. 'They are very honest and hardworking.' And then, feeling that he was somewhat disloyal to his own religion, he quickly added: 'Of course I like the sons of Catholic priests as well.' He stopped, realising that what he had just said wasn't quite right and laughed heartily. This little anecdote amused my father all his life.

Eventually, Dr Monszpart said: 'Look son, I like you. We need a paediatrician in the hospital. Go and find your family, get your papers sorted, and when you are ready, there is a place for you here. '

Food, bath, an offer of a position in this peaceful little market town and Szeged being only a day away, my parents felt life could hardly be any better. The long wilderness years were coming to a close.

It took another twelve months before my father could 'get his papers sorted'. Innocent as it sounds now, what was meant by the phrase back then was that everyone who wanted to get any job had to place an advertisement in specified papers, announcing the intention and asking for any comments from anyone. Assertions were thoroughly investigated if it was alleged that the person had either Nazi connections, or had been involved in anti-communist activities as well as criminal convictions of any kind. It could have meant a lengthy legal battle, even prison, just to prove one's innocence. Of course, the practice was wide open for personal vendettas and bribery. Neither was it a cheap process.

'Here,' said my grandmother the next day, now

all of us safely in Szeged, 'have this.' She unhooked her necklace. The price of the advertisement, as it turned out, was six centimetres of finely worked, heavy gold chain.

Nobody had anything to say but praise for my father, and in 1947 he took on the task of establishing a paediatric unit at Kiskunhalas hospital.

A copy of a document survived amongst my father's papers, dated 30 March 1946. It must have been instrumental in securing the position in Kiskunhalas. Its sheer survival indicates the importance. It was written by the retiring National Chair of Hungarian Paediatricians, currently Director of Budapest Madarász utca Children's Hospital, Dr Paul Kemény. He must have been an important and influential man, holding these positions.

It reads:

I, the undersigned Dr Paul Kemény, in full knowledge of my legal responsibility state the following: I do know Dr Dezső Gyüre. I worked with the above mentioned in Ungvár Hospital from March 22 1943 till December 30 1943. I served there in the Jewish work battalion* as a medical doctor. While in Ungvár I was assigned mostly to other wards but for two weeks I worked on Dr Gyüre's ward, as his deputy. During my whole stay in Ungvár he behaved towards me, and, as far as I *know, with every other work battalion doctor as an impeccable colleague. As we are both paediatricians, our frequent consultations concerned medical matters. But he often joined the discussions of other work battalion colleagues in the doctors' dining room. I can't comment about his political leanings, since we never touched on political matters. I could only deduce from the odd remark that he deeply opposed the war.*

He always showed the utmost care, understanding and selflessness towards patients, irrespective of their social standing, nationality or religious beliefs. His preference was to treat everyone free of charge, not just his hospital patients but his own private patients too. He even passed on the fee which some patients elected to pay for private rooms to his subordinate colleagues. He certainly showed socialist* behaviour as a person in charge. As far as I know he never conducted any kind of political activity. As I left the Ungvár Hospital on the 30th December 1943 I have no knowledge of his activities in 1944.

Signed by Dr Paul Kemény and two witnesses.

*It needs an explanation for modern readers. 'Work battalion' meant that these doctors were all Jewish. They were called up to serve in the army (on Hitler's side!) but instead of being sent to the front, they were assigned to serve according to their qualification.

'Socialist behaviour' also has a specific meaning in the context. It means that although he wasn't a communist party member, he was the next best thing because his actions showed that he was a socialist in principles, therefore not against the regime.

Kiskunhalas Hospital, 1950s. Note the obligatory communist star.

Doctors of Kiskunhalas Hospital, sitting: my father first left, Dr Monszpart third from left. 1950.

The Violin

1875 – 1927

I have a violin, out of sight, buried deep behind the winter coats in the hall. It is not particularly valuable; it isn't even in good condition. What's more I don't play any musical instruments at all. Logic says that it should have been given away a long time ago. I keep it still because it was precious to my mother. Throughout my childhood it sat as a brooding presence, forever untouched, in the half-light, on the top of her wardrobe. It was the spare violin of her father, whom I have never known. He played it. It came with him from Transylvania.

His story of how he came to leave Transylvania and live and work in Szeged is full of sadness, immeasurable loss, but bravery too.

Let's stop here for a moment.

I just said: Transylvania. What is your immediate association? Do you think of Count Dracula, rising from the dead? Do you see malevolent, mystic, bloodsucking monsters, swirls of mist, shadowy hills and gloomy castles? And you think that you are in the never-never land of Transylvania? Surely all those shiveringly wonderful vampire movies couldn't be all wrong!

They are. The source is much closer to home, because the avalanches of films were based on 19th century Irish gothic writer, Bram Stoker's novel. He in turn relied on ancient Irish mythology, according to which Dreach Fhoula (pronounced Drac Ula, meaning Tainted Blood) had an unsavoury habit of rising from his grave and needing to drink blood. He also had a fortress, Dun Dreach Fhoula, guarding a treacherous pass in the Macgillycuddy Reeks Mountains in Co. Kerry. In fact, shape-shifting, malevolent, blood-drinking evil spirits are still in current folklore in various parts of Ireland. Why Stoker decided to shift the location to Transylvania is unknown, he never visited there.

There is however Bran Castle in Romania, near Brasov, which is wildly advertised in tourist brochures as Dracula's. It belongs to Archduke Dominik von Hapsburg, who spent his happy childhood there. He is rather irritated with all this unlooked-for attention. Why focus on invention, he claimed publicly, when the castle has its own rich history?

But you can't blame the Romanian tourist business for embracing such an international money-making opportunity. In the 14th century Romanian King Vlad the Impaler lived at Bran, a sadistic ruler, whose cruelty knew no bounds. Nothing much to celebrate perhaps but the castle looks the part, has a convenient number of romantic looking turrets, ancient walls, secret passageways, mountains in the background, and to complete the tourist experience a few hauntings are easily arranged.

No Hungarian associates Transylvania with Dracula. I only became conscious of the power of connection in the mind of the 'outside world' when I came to live in Britain and innocently happened to mention to casual acquaintances that my family came from Transylvania. A tiresome nudge-nudge usually followed, with witticisms on the theme of how 'vampire-ish' I might be. I gave up protesting when I realized that no amount of earnest explanation has the power to negate those potent movie images.

However there IS a real Transylvania. It now belongs to Romania.

If you look on the map it is east of present-day Hungary, it is the area enclosed by the sickle shaped Carpathian mountain range. It is beautiful countryside, with snow-capped Alpine mountains, vast forests, lush meadows, generous vineyards, fast flowing clean rivers and profitable mines. Think of Switzerland and the Black Forest, and you get the flavour of the region, dotted by lovely ancient towns and charming villages. Since around 800 AD, ever since Hungary as a state existed, it was part of Hungary.

Transylvania was originally settled by the Seklers, short, stocky, hardy mountain people, whose role has always been to defend the Eastern borders of Hungary. Seklers were famous for their wit, ingenuity and honesty. For us to be a Sekler was, and still is a 'passport' for respect. The oldest folklore, the most ancient songs and customs were kept alive in Transylvania, and the purest Hungarian language was spoken there.

Everything came to an abrupt end with the First World War. Being part of the Austro-Hungarian Empire inevitably meant that we were German allies. Not that we had much against the Germans. In the Hungarian mind, through Protestantism, Germany long represented education, enlightenment, hard work and unquestionable loyalty. When the chips were down, Hungarians went willingly to war; they saw it as their national duty. The Europe-wide fervour, so well documented in Britain, infected us too. The euphoria did not last long, as it didn't anywhere else either. Our casualties were crippling.

The First World War ended in 1918, but for us peace was even more cataclysmic. In 1920 at Trianon, the Allied Forces, i.e. the United States, the British Empire, France and Italy, dictated the non-negotiable terms of the peace treaty. Country boundaries were re-drawn. Of the former Hungarian territory only 28 per cent was left, the rest was allocated mostly to Romania, Czechoslovakia and

Yugoslavia. Of our ten major towns only five remained Hungarian and 31 per cent of the population now lived outside our boundaries. The whole of Transylvania and a goodly chunk of the Eastern Hungarian plains now became Romanian. This 'truncation' hurt then and it still hurts, a hundred years later. I think you have to be Hungarian to understand the magnitude of the loss.

Imagine though, just for a moment, that Britain was somehow conquered and it was declared that Warwickshire, Worcestershire, Gloucestershire, Oxfordshire, Berkshire, and Wiltshire were no longer English. Your mother tongue would be forbidden, all official communication would be in another language. If you wanted to travel from Manchester to Birmingham or to Oxford, you needed to get a passport. Imagine how, a generation or two later, families, now living in other parts of Britain would recall once familiar place names like Dorchester, Kelmscott, Shipton-under-Wychwood, Cirencester or Littlewick Green, all renamed now. Tearfully, they would savour the sweetness of those lost sounds, recall the old home, the ancient church and the unvisited cemetery. It never happened here, but that is what happened in Hungary.

With a stroke of a pen some vital parts of our country were gone. The nation wilted like a plant when its main tap root is severed, and started to create new, subsidiary roots. As a desperate attempt to salvage whatever is salvageable, it was decided that the University of Kolozsvár (Cluj, to give it its Romanian name) must move, lock, stock and barrel, to somewhere within the new Hungarian borders. (Think in parallel to Oxford, what would or could the institution do if its position became untenable?) The comparison is not an idle one. The University of Kolozsvár was a famous seat of learning, founded by Regent Count István Báthory in 1581, one of the first of Hungary's universities. It was also here that Protestantism first took root and became the epicentre of resistance in the 18th and 19th centuries against the Austrian imperial expansions.

My grandfather studied medicine in Hungarian Kolozsvár. He was an immensely gifted and diligent student. When he gained his medical degree in 1900, Emperor Franz Joseph personally presented him with a diamond-encrusted ring, an honour bestowed on the most outstanding student in the whole of Hungary. (The ring is now in possession of my eldest cousin Anikó.) After his degree he studied in Vienna, Tübingen, Berlin, Dresden and Leipzig and later, as an acclaimed authority, he also visited Oxford. Ground-breaking research in the new science, biochemistry, saw him as still quite a young man, become professor at his old university, Kolozsvár.

He married my grandmother there. Kolozsvár was a wonderful place to live. Steeped in history and tradition, it was lively, well-to-do and intellectually exciting, set in a magically beautiful alpine landscape. My grandparents were happy, settled, financially at ease, he was successful in work, they had two healthy, intelligent children, a boy and a girl, and they were surrounded by a loving, wider family.

It was not to last.

Scarlet fever took both the children within days of each other. The First World War itself wasn't as traumatic as it could have been for the family, because my grandfather, as a distinguished academic, was not called up. None of the family suffered any casualties either. The real tragedy came with the peace treaty, in 1920. Transylvania was NOT Hungarian any more. The decision was taken: save the university! It was argued that the essence of a university is generated by the excellence of its staff and the traditions and ethos these people embody. Location, bricks and stones are secondary. They believed that they could have Kolozsvár University somewhere else.

I see it almost as a part of science fiction, something like this: forced to leave Earth, which is now for them uninhabitable, a band of people, men, women and children are transported in a capsule to alien lands, away from the clean air of high mountains, to a flat, hot, dusty planet to start life again. This life will resemble their previous life but it can never again be the same.

It was no fiction, though, it happened. Forty-two families, all senior academic staff, left the ancient

University of Kolozsvár in 1921 and relocated to Szeged. Dr Béla Reinbold, my mother's father, Professor of Biochemistry, and his family were amongst the sad group of academics who made the journey. What it must have cost them in emotional terms, God only knows.

Meanwhile Kolozsvár became Cluj Napoca and King Ferdinand inaugurated the new Romanian University of Cluj in 1920.

At least Szeged meant Hungary; and the city was delighted to welcome them. It also has to be said that Szeged was never the same again either, this influx of Protestant and Jewish academics brought with them probing intellectual vistas, high ideals, literature, art and music, which complemented the Catholic ethos of the prosperous agricultural city. In time the newcomers learned to like the glowing red, greasy, devilishly hot paprika fish soup, signature dish of their new home.

Szeged and the university in time became one. Famous for its academic excellence to this day, the 'space travellers' became part of history. Unobserved and disregarded in the Stefánia Park though, by the tranquil banks of the Tisza River, there are some strange boulders dotted around. They are so perfectly smooth and round, that it is difficult to believe that they are not man-made but formed by volcanic action in the far away Hargita Mountains, in Transylvania. The forty-two families brought them – symbolically bringing the very ground of their home with them.[1]

There was a lot of work to be done. The 1920s economic climate was difficult, the political situation unstable and the whole nation mourned the lost territories. The ex-Transylvanians kept close to each other and heroically did their best. This bond amongst them was so strong that even now, grandchildren and great-grandchildren still know each other.

Professor Béla Reinbold created and directed the Szeged Institute of Medical Biochemistry. His research interests concerned degradation of carbohydrates in the body, amongst other things the detection of carbohydrates in the urine. He became Vice Chancellor of the University in 1922-23 and again in 1927-28.

Perhaps an indication of the standards of research which my grandfather established is that Albert Szentgyörgyi, discoverer of vitamin C, worked at his institute and was later awarded the Nobel Prize.

I know so very little about him as a man. I think my grandmother and he were a very happy couple. I do know that his daughters adored him.

A received memory drifts past.

---

[1] I am sure the stones are a Biblical reference to Joshua Chapter 4, verse 3 *Take you...twelve stones and ye shall carry them over with you.*

In the scented June evening in 1906, Kolozsvár is dreamily still. Tall, dark-haired, blue-eyed Ida Muller is stepping out with handsome Béla Reinbold; his sister and her brother are already engaged. He is quiet, almost serious. He plucks a flower from the Indian bean tree and says, 'Iduska, you are as beautiful as this flower.' (The flower is something like a conker tree flower, subtly off white, with delicate maroon veins, not at all showy, not at all obvious.) Delighted in the compliment, she hugged it to herself and kept it forever. When she told me the story, over fifty years later, those flowers, that June evening were still with her. And I retell the story with some resigned envy. How I wish that somebody told me, told me in such a way that I could believe it – that I am that beautiful.

Their amusements must have been quiet. In the first year of their marriage in the evenings they knotted a 'Persian' carpet. It is still breathtakingly wonderful, on the wall of my Manchester home.

When we were children, in bed, and only when ill, my mother used to tell us the *Thermometer Story*. It goes like this:

When God first created the birds, they had no colour at all. He looked at them and thought he could make them much more beautiful, so he called all the birds to come, to line up to get painted. All the birds came, with little beaks and big beaks, short and tall, and God, with his enormous palette and innumerable colours, painted them all. A bit of red here, a dab of yellow there, some in one colour, some spotted. The birds left one by one, being very proud of their wonderful new outfits.

Towards the end of the day God was getting tired. All the birds were painted now and he was about to wash out his brushes. Suddenly he heard a little crying 'cheep!' He looked around, but could see nothing. Cheep! Again, and a sob. He saw a tiny little bird, unpainted, miserable. 'Why did you not come when I called you?' thundered God.

'I did come,' chirruped the little bird miserably, 'but I am so little that the big birds pushed me away – and now I am going to be the only bird in all Kingdom who is colourless.'

God said. 'Look, all the paint is gone. I am finished.' But he thought and smiled. 'I know what I will do. There is still paint in all of my brushes, and there is paint left on my palette too. Come here little bird, I will wipe out my brushes on you.'

So the little bird had a dash of pink and bright green and yellow, he had spots of turquoise and stripes of summer sky blue and he became the most beautiful bird in the world. He was so very happy and God was happy too.

And this is the end of the story.

It was called the thermometer story in the family because it had to last five minutes while the thermometer in the crook of your armpit measured whether you were ill or not. My mother used to hold us the same way as her father used to hold her and tell her the self-same story.

What I did not know when I was listening to the story, feeling snug and safe, that my mother and her two sisters were the second 'clutch' of children for my grandparents. In 1908 they had a little girl, Edit and in 1911 a boy, József. In 1915 both contracted scarlet fever and all the knowledge of the professor of medicine, eminent scholar, was useless. The children died within two days of each other.

That is when they decided to have more children and along came Ilma, my mother (1916), Anci (1918), and Alice (1921).

Holding and measuring the temperature of one of his feverish little girls later, reassuringly telling them about God and birds must have masked terrible possibilities in his mind. It just shows how good he must have been that neither my mother nor I had ever had an inkling of this anxiety. Only love and safety.

Alice was only one year old when they had to leave Kolozsvár. The task of establishing a new university and continuing the research demanded long hours. There was no public transport, so he walked an hour from home and an hour back again. His family lived for the time when he was at home, which was not that often, for Professor Reinbold drove himself almost beyond endurance. In the evenings the children, already in bed, heard the quiet chat of their parents through half-closed doors, and after that invariably wonderful violin music. Making music was his way of being at peace again.

It was like this one December evening in 1927. Serenity reigned as he played Schumann's *Träumerei*. My mother listened drowsily, her sisters were already asleep. Abruptly the music stopped. Then there were loud, confused noises, sudden commotion in the next room, strange voices. 'Heart attack', she heard, 'he is gone'.

She understood it with blinding clarity. 'I am fatherless,' she registered to herself and the next thought came: 'I am the oldest child. From now on I will have to be mother's support.'

She was only twelve. No wonder the violin was so dear to her.

Next day my grandfather, as VC, was meant to make the speech at the graduation ceremony of the new doctors. It was already written and it was read out to the stunned grandaunts. It became his obituary. His message was: 'Whatever path your life might take, look for the truth and follow the truth. If you manage to uncover just one, small, hitherto unknown truth about the world, you will be a contented man.'

He was just fifty-two. My grandmother never again wore anything else but black.

Next time, when you are asked by an efficient nurse, 'Can you please give us a urine sample in this bottle?' just think: It was that shooting star, the brilliant, passionate, romantic Professor Béla Reinbold, my grandfather, whose research contributed to making the painless test possible.

Béla, Ella, Klotild (Oliver's three children), *cc*1882.

Béla, as a young man, *cc*1895

The diamond ring with Emperor Franz Joseph's initials presented to Béla, the outstanding student, on receiving his medical degree.

The girl who looked like the flower of the Indian bean tree. Our grandmother, Ida cc1900.

With their two children, Edit and József in Kolozsvar, 1915. These are the children who died. The two creases on the photo indicate that it must have been carried in a valet – I presume by Béla, the father. If Ida folded it, she would not have chopped her husband's face in half.

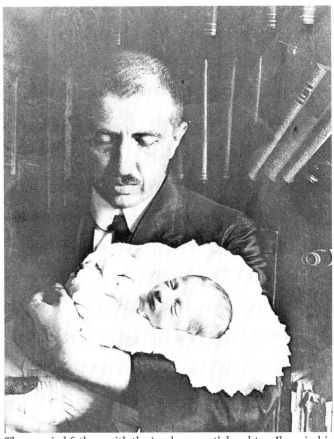

The worried father, with the 'replacement' daughter, Ilma, in his study. 1916.

The stones from Transylvania's Hargita Mountain, in a Szeged park.

The last ever picture of him in Szeged. The professor is very tired. 1927.

Family Beginnings

A portrait, painted cc1835-40

Béla's successes did not grow out of nothing. A long family path led him to his eventual achievements. Perhaps now is the time to take a stroll back through the centuries on to these winding lanes, much covered and overgrown but still discernible. A darkish portrait, hanging all alone, frameless but imposing, is our lead. It is not a junkshop find, bought to fill in an empty space. It belonged to my grandparents and as the eldest child of an eldest child it came to me. A very staid and dignified middle-aged man, with all the trappings of learnedness looks at me, without a hint of what he might be thinking or feeling. I stared at him as a child, searching, willing him to speak, but he gave nothing away.

Not his fault. You have to be a very good portrait painter to communicate the personality of the sitter, rather than the physical features. Rembrandt could do it, and Reynolds, Picasso and many others. The portrait that I have in my house is not one of these.

Still, he is my great-great-great-grandfather, Dr Ignaz Reinbold.

Ignaz, portrait, *cc*1835-40

How lucky, though, to have the portrait at all! There is more, too, as Ignaz was an avid diary writer, who drew as well. All these precious, unique family documents survived against all the odds. My mother's cousin, Mihály, rescued them from the family estates during the Second World War. He stitched the documents into the lining of his winter coat as he was fleeing when it became clear that Transylvania would never again be Hungary. He looked after them until 1987 and just before his death he presented the collection for safekeeping to the Hungarian National Archives.

What is clear, looking at these documents, is that this balding, sober gentleman was not always old, was not always staid; he was also dashing and daring, colourful, even reckless in his youth, like the times he lived in, during the Napoleonic wars.

His diaries describe a world, alien and familiar to us at the same time. Reading them is like visiting a foreign land, where customs and speech are alien until you realise that our concerns are the same.

He was born to a mother of restricted circumstances in 1774, his father died before he was born. He spent his childhood in a monastery boarding school, where, besides an excellent education, he seems to have received some affection as well. At nineteen he joined the army, fighting Napoleon as a trainee medic.

As formal studies were restricted to only those times when his unit happened to be stationed in Vienna, it took him sixteen years to qualify. He finally gained his ordinary medical degree as well as the additional specialist surgeon's qualifications at the Joseph Academy in 1808. Meanwhile, he married in 1802 in Transylvania.

As a family man, army life didn't suit him

anymore. By 1810 he managed to pay off the army and with great dedication he applied himself to his civilian life. His energies were divided between his hospital duties, private patients, managing and enlarging the, by now considerable, estates and the education of his sons. From his six children, only two sons, Josef and Anton, and a daughter reached adulthood. Both sons went on to higher education to study law and mining engineering. He also found it imperative that his sons should have a wider outlook, and financed their foreign study tours.

Josef, the elder son and our ancestor, spent a year in Hungary, Poland, Silesia, Moravia, Austria and Bohemia to complete his education, returning in 1830. The Europe-wide revolutions of 1848 were catastrophic for the German- and Hungarian-speaking Reinbold family. Seeing themselves firmly as monarchist landowners, they had no sympathy either with the Hungarian efforts to shake off Austrian rule or with the independence-seeking and vengeful Romanians.

Ignaz's house was looted and burned down; the whole family ran to hide in the wild forests, chased by the angry Romanian mob. They caught up with Anton, his younger son, and brutally murdered him, but not before Anton himself tried to shoot his wife and two daughters to save them from a 'fate worse than death'. Luckily his aim wasn't too good. That is how Ignaz found them, Anton dead, his wife and daughters bleeding and in shock. They did survive.

Though Ignaz rebuilt his house; he couldn't ever rebuild his life. Poor old Ignaz, he was a true man of the Enlightenment, he rarely allowed emotions to interfere with reason. A loyal soldier, a dedicated doctor of medicine, he always tried so very hard, doing his best, never deviating from the path of what he saw as his duty. His actions and his diaries show him to be meticulous, educated, honest, and intelligent. Starting with nothing, he built, brick by brick, a life and a position for himself and for his family. Writing and drawing, as always, provided some refuge. He died in 1851.

His diaries give us a rare glimpse into times we only know from history books, describing a life far removed from ours. They start in his youth, when the balding gentleman of the portrait was young, dashing and daring.

As a trainee medic of the Austrian army, twenty-six-year-old Ignaz Reinbold is ordered to collect and transport 120 injured soldiers by sea from Genoa to Pisa. He is accompanied by a corporal and three privates from his regiment and is given three Italian commercial ships with an Italian crew to accomplish the task. The year is 1800, when the allied Austrian, German and Italian armies and the English navy were trying to halt Napoleon's European expansionist plans. General Massena's French army seized the port of Genoa after bitter fighting. They were surrounded, however, by Austrian troops on land and blockaded from the sea by the English fleet, led by Admiral Lord Keith.

Wounded Austrian men were trapped in Genoa, but Massena granted permission for them to be evacuated. It did not seem too difficult a task; according to Ignaz's diaries he was looking forward to the mission. In preparation for the manoeuvre Ignaz acquired old cotton items for bandages as well as bread and rusks in Sestri Ponente and sailed on to Voltri, where he purchased salt, wine, water, meat and rice.

So on the twenty-third of May in the evening, we sailed off into the open sea. I made myself comfortable in my cabin and spun sweet plans about this expedition. I felt that I was one of the luckiest men alive, I prepared bandages, I had food and drink to hand and eventually went to sleep with the most pleasurable dreams, from which I was awoken by a shot.

I cautiously peeped out from my hidey-hole and saw right in front of my nose a boat, with some sailors, demanding to know why I am swimming about here. Judging from their speech they were English but I could only communicate with them in Italian.

They ordered my crew to sail in a certain direction until we saw a flag, signalling the ship of the admiral.

It was daybreak and my curiosity was sky-high. I noticed some light above the endless clear waterline, with some dark dots here and there. The mountain range of Savona and Genoa were hardly visible any more when these dots changed into the widely dispersed boats of the English fleet. I could hear bells and music by 8 o'clock in the morning so I assumed the admiral must be on board. The air and water were quiet so I could get close to the contraption, with the twenty-one and a half battalion guns pointing right at me.

From below I showed them my papers and they pointed at a ladder for me to climb up. At the admiral's quarters, which had great glass windows and doors, I handed him my papers. The top deck was freshly scrubbed and covered with carpets; officers and sailors strolled everywhere. I was permitted to wander all over the place, to look at everything, admire the vessel, the structure of the standing and struck down masts, the complicated rigging, the large triangular and square sails. I saw the steersman by the wheel with his compass and the Bo'sun. The latter has a whistle of such penetrating sound that all the sailors by the ropes are able to hear him. Orders are given with these signals and the sails can change shape in an instant. I was offered, but declined the chance of clambering up to the crow's nest on the main mast, it swayed noticeably though the weather was calm and we were hardly listing. What happens when there is a storm?

After I passed the seventy-two heavy cannons on small cylindrical wheels, I wanted to see the levels *below deck, the store rooms, the hospital and the place where the seamen sleep. This last one consisted of nets, fastened at either end to the ceiling. One could lie in the nets but when not in use and rolled up, they were hardly bigger than the size of two fists.*

While I was walking wordlessly among these English, a messenger was sent to the commanders of Genoa that my three ships must be allowed to reach the harbour unhindered. I set sail around midday but within an hour a sudden storm came. It was impossible to stay standing on the deck, unless hanging on to the mast and I feared that the wild waves would swallow us. Suddenly there came a hollow thud, above the boat into the water. They were shooting at us from Genoa!

I was petrified and my heart was beating wildly. I wasn't thinking of the storm any more, the cannonballs gave me something else to think about. I rushed down into my cabin and, not wishing to become fish food, sitting among my old, torn up linen I devised a plan. Should our ship be hit I would stuff the holes with balls made from the bandages!

Suddenly there was another shot, but this time from right behind us from an English frigate. I just couldn't comprehend what this might mean. There was no power on earth which would make me get out of my cabin. But my Italian crew was cleverer than me; they turned sail and in no time at all we were back at the admiral's ship. It turned out that the English were watching our lack of progress with their telescope from the flagship and came to our rescue. They lowered three barges from those leaning masts with twelve oarsmen on each, attached ropes to our ships and towed us unhindered into the harbour.

We were allowed to land at the lighthouse as the sun was setting. There, waiting for us, as if for the Messiah were the 120 wretched men, wounded, starving and in pain. While they were transported into three ships I would have liked to have seen something of Genoa, rumoured to be a splendid city, but was denied access. I could attend to the moaning injured at last, moving on a small boat from ship to ship. It was well into the night when all were taken care of, the sea was calm once more and we could all rest at last. The two dead were buried at sea.

It appears that what Ignaz thought was going to be a pleasurable cruising adventure turned out to be quite a journey.

He was no sailor, this much is clear. It is odd reading his diary, almost listening to his voice that he saw the real, working predecessor of *HMS Victory*, that he actually talked to Admiral Lord Keith, Nelson's rival, that he did not know about hammocks and that he thought he could save a gun-torn ship by plugging the hole with rolled up linen bandages.

I can just see him wandering around on the

magnificent flagship and calling it a contraption, for he had no word to describe this efficient war machine, counting the number of guns, which he got wrong, trying to figure out how things operated, looking at the construction, while the rough English sailor lads nudged each other, sniggering behind his back and trying to send this haughty, poncy German up to the crow's nest for a laugh.

All we know of the rest of the journey is that he took the wounded on board in Genoa on the twenty-third of May and arrived, shortly before daybreak on June the second in Pisa. It could not have been plain sailing.

The bells tolled at sunrise and those who could walk got off the ships. All of a sudden a group of men, dressed in long black gowns and hoods appeared. Their whole faces were covered too, just with holes for their eyes. They had stretchers with them and carried all the injured to the hospital. It was hot and heavy work, so occasionally they lifted the hood, took off their gloves, sometimes you could see their shoes. It became obvious that these were upper class, rich men, as diamond rings and shoe buckles glittered. I was told that they all belong to a Fraternity – that is laymen, affiliated to monastery, who volunteered to take care of any sick and injured according to a well-organised rota.

Together we placed the injured in the hospital

and I sent my staff back to their regiment. But I took myself off and found a nice little comfortable inn way out of town. Next morning I went to see Pisa, where I found a massive tower, built in an odd way, slanting about twelve feet from the centre.

This is just one of the many undertakings described in his diary, for his path was eventful by all accounts, full of unexpected twist and turns.

How could I get to know him?

I have decided that all I have to do is ask. I imagined him sitting next to me. (His answers are either direct quotes from his diaries or what I presume to read between the lines.)

It is an odd experience to 'talk' to an ancestor whom you have never met. In the immediate family, we all know the feeling of highlighting the differences between us and tending to say things like 'I do this, but my sister would do that' or 'My parents believed such and such yet I choose something else.' We need this to assert our own individuality and to take pride in making our own path through life.

Yet from a distance, from a stranger's point of view, the physical or psychological similarities are much more pronounced than the differences. 'They all have that nose!' people might comment or, 'I am not surprised little Jimmy is top of the class, look how hard-working his whole family is.'

I have the stranger's distance from Ignaz, the

distance of time and language and his whole view of the world. I am trying to use this distance to seek out the familial similarities, to try to understand him from the inside. He was alive once, as I am alive now. Through his descendants, through me, parts of him are alive still.

This is how the conversation went:

Ilma: Dr Reinbold, I am your great-great–great-granddaughter, how may I address you?

Ignaz: Just call me Ignaz. You are part of me and I am part of you. Nothing I say to you can be that alien; you'll see, you'll recognise yourself. Not only that, you might find attitudes and even physical features in the wider family which will bring me to mind.

Ilma: How did you become a doctor and a soldier? I thought you wanted to be a monk!

Ignaz: Now there is a story! Quite by accident in fact.

As you know, my mother was from the ancient family of von Hundt, with a knightly estate. Unfortunately, by our time the income from this was meagre. Any further study after I left the monastery at eighteen was out of the question. As I still wanted to return to the safety and familiarity of dear Allerheiligen, I devised an excellent plan. I would become a pharmacist, apprenticed to our local apothecary Mr Bosiers, and I reckoned when I qualified I would be able to return. I was diligent and useful to this rude and quick-tempered man, but I had had enough when he shouted at me just because I accidentally broke some phials. And in front of all the Saturday customers, who all knew me! Nobody can talk to me like that! I thought. So I turned on my heels and swore never to return.

Ilma: When was all this?

Ignaz: 1792. The French, led by Napoleon, had just declared war against Austria. Don't forget, in my time the area where we lived by the Rhine was part of Western Austria. Soldiers began to march and Austrian troops were settling above Speyer. That was exciting! Of course I was curious; I had nothing better to do and being bored and penniless I just took myself off to spend a week in the soldiers' camp. When I mentioned my pharmaceutical experiences someone suggested that I should join the army as an orderly. Although I knew absolutely nothing of surgery and less about pharmacy they took me as a new practising army recruit medic on June eighth, in the nineteenth year of my life.

Ilma: How did you start your training? Was it hard?

Ignaz: I was posted to the Dominican Order's Field Hospital in Heidelberg, under Dr Metzger, and saw some action immediately. I remained there for nine months and survived it in good health, apart from a minor injury. But it was not always just danger and hard work! We enjoyed life too. Here in the cellar of the castle of Heidelberg is an enormous barrel, put there quite recently in 1751. It holds 2,884 buckets and on top of the barrel there is a platform with railings, big enough for six couples to dance on. I believe people in your time still come to see it and you would now say that it holds 220,000 litres.

Ilma: Yes, I have seen it too as a tourist attraction. Funny, we venerate the barrel as something old; in your time it was still a novelty.

How did you get on as a doctor?

Ignaz: I learned fast, from the other doctors. Within two years, in 1794, I was officially appointed as a 'sub-doctor' with a comfortable salary of fifteen florin and of course full board. I was assigned to the battalion of Count Sámuel Gyulay, a Hungarian Transylvanian. In fact, I stayed mainly with the Hungarian regiments all through my soldier's career.

Ilma: Of course, as part of the Austro-Hungarian Empire, Hungarians fought alongside the Austrians.

Did it feel strange to you to be surrounded by Hungarians?

Ignaz: Not at all, everyone spoke German in any case. You see the Empire was so colourful, with so many different nationalities mingling with each other, not just Hungarian and Austrian but Czech, Croat, Italian, Polish, Romanian, Ruthenian, Serbian, Slovak, Slovene, just to mention the most numerous ones. And, as I said, everyone spoke German.

Ilma: Were you always stationed in Heidelberg?

Ignaz: Oh no, not at all! With my regiment we marched up and down, criss-crossing Europe. We fought and endured dangers and hardships, in territories now known as North and South Germany, Belgium, Eastern France, Luxemburg, The Netherlands, Austria, Croatia, Serbia, Italy, Hungary, Transylvania and Romania. Mind, my regiment never got further than Europe, but people fought against Napoleon in Egypt and Russia too.

Ilma: I don't quite understand. So where was this war?

Ignaz: Don't think of it as one war, more like a series of wars, fought by an ever-changing pattern of allies, interspersed with lulls and truces. There was only one constant factor, that the French were the aggressors. It did start by Napoleon declaring war on the Austrian Empire but it spread all over Europe and beyond.

Ilma: Someone of my time would inevitably think about your time as the age of heady, revolutionary new ideas. Liberty, fraternity, equality are intoxicating concepts. Were you affected by them at all?

Ignaz: I did not think about it overmuch but no, oh no! They attempted to abolish everything I felt to be sacrosanct, the existing order, the social hierarchy and the monasteries. Even Allerheiligen! Look at Napoleon; do you think he believed in equality?

Men are not born equal. There has to be a

structure and ours has worked well for centuries.

Ilma: So, did you enjoy the fighting? Is that why you joined?

Ignaz: Not the fighting, no. I liked being a doctor but occasionally hated the fighting. I even tried to desert the army once by pretending to be lost and wounded in a forest, but my comrades found me and 'rescued' me. By joining the army I hoped to see more of the world. Indeed, wherever we went I made sure that I saw everything I could. Of course I also realised that being a military doctor was a route to prove myself, to become respected and prosperous. Meanwhile I had exciting adventures. I could tell you some things!

Ilma: What did you see?

Ignaz: Well now, what did I see? So many wondrous things!

Köln has a leaning tower. Legend has it that when they brought the body of the Three Kings to the city, the tower bowed out of respect. There are 365 towers here but I couldn't see them all. And in Rastadt Castle garden the statue of Jupiter is as tall as a man and it is covered in pure gold.

You know what they say about Freiburg? We all laughed when we heard it! The ditty goes like this:

Freyburg eine schone Stadt
hat einen Thurm ohne Dach
in jedrer Gass einen Bach:
auf jedem Thor eine Uhr:
in jedem Haus eine Hur:

Freiburg is a pretty town
Has a tower without a roof,
In every street a brook
On every gate a clock,
In every house a whore.

Ilma: Does this mean that by that time you had given up all thoughts of becoming a monk and you joined in in all the 'soldierly' pursuits?

Ignaz: A gentleman does not answer questions like these! However, Schwetzingen Castle's garden has artificial ruins, a minaret, a bathhouse with mirrors, labyrinth bridges, paintings with beautiful perspectives and magical water plays, where the hidden machinery is driven out of sight by convicts.

Ilma: You know, in my time we find using convicts to power machinery just to amuse the nobility quite shocking.

Ignaz: I don't see why. There are windmills and watermills, but if they are not suitable there is only the strength of animals or humans. What other power sources can there be? That reminds me that at Mons in Wallonia they often use dogs to pull small carts. There was another first for me in Wallonia; I had my first cup of coffee in nearby Namur. Right outside our barracks milky coffee was being sold by the cupful. Of course I was curious about what coffee tasted like, so I too bought a cup.

Ilma: All this is very strange for me to hear. Everyone everywhere drinks coffee nowadays. But you know, you still haven't told me how you qualified as a doctor and how you became my great great-great-grandfather!

Ignaz: Therein lies another long and complicated story but I am not going to tell you all about it here.

Read my diaries! Suffice it to say that when my regiment was stationed in Transylvania in Königsburg, you now know it as Gyulafehérvár or in Romanian Alba Julia. Here I met and married Josepha Hammerschmidt, youngest daughter of the Principal of the Royal Mint in 1802.

She came from a very well-to-do noble family. We had six children, but only three lived beyond infancy: Josef Ignaz, your great-great-grandfather, Anton and Johanna Napomucena.

As I distinguished myself in service, I was allowed formal study in Vienna University whenever we were stationed there, and eventually gained a medical degree, specializing in surgery, in 1808. It took me sixteen years to finally be able to call myself qualified! I applied for a civilian post in Transylvania, in Zalatna soon afterwards and left the army for good.

Ilma: I know that my grandfather, Dr Béla Reinbold is known as Borosbenedeki Reinbold, which means that he was part of the Hungarian titled nobility. How did that come about? You yourself did not have a title.

Ignaz: No, I did not. But I have always earned well and was also meticulous with finances. Josepha had considerable wealth, title and land to which I added significantly. Based on my services to the Crown and our position I started petitioning in1838 to be accepted to the ranks of the Transylvanian nobility. It was something I felt we were owed and I was stubborn, renewing my petition again and again to be heard at the highest authority. However, in spite of promises, the decision was always deferred. The political climate was complicated and I appreciated that his majesty, Franz Joseph, had more important matters to consider.

Josef, my son, your great-great-grandfather, continued the petitioning after my death, but to no avail. He also married well, to a Hungarian lady, the noble Emilia Árkosy of Dálnok, who inherited the estate at Borosbenedek. Their eight children were brought up as Hungarian.

Oliver, his only his son, your great-grandfather, eventually succeeded in attaining the long family ambition, and on his retirement as royal adviser he was granted the noble title Borosbenedeki, and the right to the family shield in 1898.

Allerheiligen now, nothing but a romantic ruin.

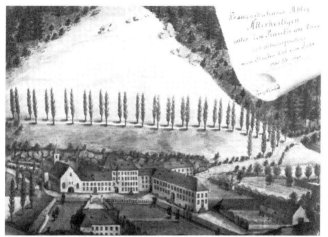

Ignaz's student drawing of Allerheiligen.

Ignaz's drawing of an excursion in Transylvania, showing himself looking backwards. 1810.

Some of Ignaz's drawings.

Legacy and Family Pretensions

This preoccupation with nobility in the family, still something of a silent force even in my mother's generation, puzzled me as a child, growing up as I did in communist Hungary. It undoubtedly harks back to Ignaz.

His diary starts: I, Ignaz Reinbold was born in Unterachern in Breissgau, by the Rheine, on 15th of December, 1774.

His mother was Josepha von Hundt, the daughter of Johann Georg von Hundt and Catharina Gutmannin. The von Hundts were apparently descendants of German knights but now almost penniless. Ignaz's father was the Kellermeister, Master of the Cellars in Karlsruhe at the princely seat of the Margrave of Baden, Karl Friedrich. Ignaz never knew his father, who died before he was born.

There is a persistent, unsubstantiated rumour in the family that not everything was as it seemed. In this version of events Ignaz's mother, who herself was from a noble but not particularly wealthy family, was a mistress of the duke. When she fell pregnant, a marriage was arranged with the ailing

Reinbold, an important member of the court's household.

Were this to be true, then there is almost no royal family in Europe he was not related to.

But if you are a descendant of Ignaz and start to imagine grandeur at this point, hang on a bit. The duke had five children from his first marriage and four from his second. He was also reputed to have had thirty mistresses. Counting thirty years as a generation and an average of two and a half children, an estimated 97,000 people to date could claim Karl Friedrich as an ancestor.

When I read Ignaz's diaries, I was looking for clues to the man, trying to get to know him. For me, as a descendant, whether he really was or was not the duke's natural son feels unimportant. I was looking for clues to see what occupied his thoughts, where he placed himself in the social hierarchy and what kind of a man these beliefs might have made him. This to me seems a much more fascinating question, at least as important as interesting tit-bits of history.

We do know that the little boy was packed off to boarding school in the Allerheiligen Premontrei Monastery, far away from anywhere, isolated deep in the Black Forest. This ancient gothic monastery had served the district as a spiritual and educational centre since the 13th century. In Ignaz's time there were sixty to seventy students there.

We know from contemporary documents that

tuition fees were very high indeed and most of the pupils were from wealthy upper-class families. His mother could certainly not afford to send him there, but it could have been Margrave Karl Friedrich footing the bill, silently acknowledging paternity. Whether Ignaz knew who paid his fees, and why, remains his secret. The only clue we have in his diary is that: *in every respect I received fatherly care there*. He could be referring to the margrave or to the kindness of the friars. In fact, he felt so much at home that he thought he might want to become a monk himself and to stay forever. Just as well he didn't, otherwise this story would never have been written.

The wise old prior, however, suggested he studied philosophy in his home town first, wait until he was eighteen and come back if he still wanted to be a monk. Allerheiligen Monastery in the Black Forest still exists, but not as Ignaz knew it.

The buildings, the 500-year-old traditions, a way of life, which seemed eternal while he was there, disappeared within a few years of him leaving. The reason for this was the so-called 'Josephinism' of the Austro-Hungarian Empire, when about one third of monastic institutions were dissolved and the riches confiscated by the State. Allerheiligen, too, was dissolved at the beginning of the new century.

Some of the valuable old sculptures were transported to Karlsruhe Castle but the rest would have been left to its fate of crumbling oblivion, had it not had a spectacular waterfall right behind it. In the early 19th century, at the height of the Romantic era, the waterfall, the isolated forest position, the hauntingly exposed mediaeval arches made the place an obligatory visit for all who enjoyed contemplating melancholy. Allerheiligen became one of the first tourist attractions of its kind in the world. And this is what it still is. We have a private glimpse though, of how Ignaz knew the buildings, as among his many surviving drawings there is one, showing his beloved Alma Mater.

Ignaz's rich life had a certain pleasing symmetry. He left his mother, Josepha, behind and married a Josepha in Transylvania. He started life in German-speaking Schwarzwald and finished in the German-speaking Königsburg, in Transylvania. Only when I visited Allerheiligen myself did I appreciate how very similar the two countries look and feel, almost interchangeable, beautiful, wooded, hilly lands. I don't think he felt an alien in Transylvania at all.

His and his son's and grandson's preoccupation with nobility seems so irrelevant now, to the modern reader. But coming from an uncertain background as he did, having an upper-class upbringing but no private means, in an age when bloodline and lineage seriously counted, the eventual acknowledgement of the status the family felt they were already entitled to, must have been a private triumph. Certainly, the women that the successive Reinbolds married all had excellent pedigrees, with family trees as long as your arm, some dating back to the 12th century, a direct bloodline to the first Hungarian 'Árpádháza' kings. I have this family tree, beautifully researched by my uncle, Mihály, the same uncle who saved and hid the diaries in the lining of his overcoat.

If I really want to celebrate Ignaz's legacy, however, it would be the emphasis placed on education and travel, still a dominant ambition amongst all his descendants. There is another trait, also discernible – the talent for visual arts. This inner need to paint, draw, sculpt or design seems to bob up in every generation, sometimes here, sometimes there in the various branches of the family. And finally, the fact that Schwarzwald and Transylvania belonged to what we now consider two very different countries might not have been so important to people living at his time. It is only strange for us, his descendants, just how accidentally we happened to become what we are: Hungarians.

Müller Family Tree

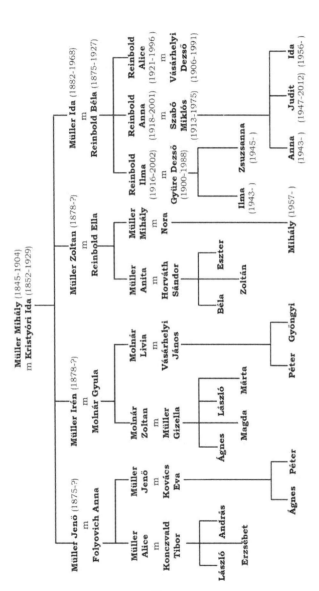

Müller Mihály (1845-1904)
m Kristyóri Ida (1852-1929)

Müller Jenő (1875-?)
m
Folyovich Anna

Müller Irén (1878-?)
m
Molnár Gyula

Müller Zoltan (1878-?)
m
Reinbold Ella

Müller Ida (1882-1968)
m
Reinbold Béla (1875-1927)

Müller Alice
m
Konczvald Tibor

Müller Jenő
m
Kovács Eva

László   András
Erzsébet

Ágnes   Péter

Molnár Zoltan
m
Müller Gizella

Molnár Lívia
m
Vásárhelyi János

Ágnes   László   Márta
Magda

Péter   Gyöngyi

Müller Anita
m
Horváth Sándor

Müller Mihály
m
Nora

Béla   Zoltán
Eszter

Mihály (1957-)

Reinbold Ilma
(1916-2002)
m
Gyüre Dezső
(1900-1988)

Reinbold Anna
(1918-2001)
m
Szabó Miklós
(1913-1975)

Reinbold Alice
(1921-1996)
m
Vásárhelyi Dezső
(1906-1991)

Ilma
(1943-)

Zsuzsanna
(1945-)

Anna
(1943-)

Judit
(1947-2012)

Ida
(1956-)

Reinbold Family Tree

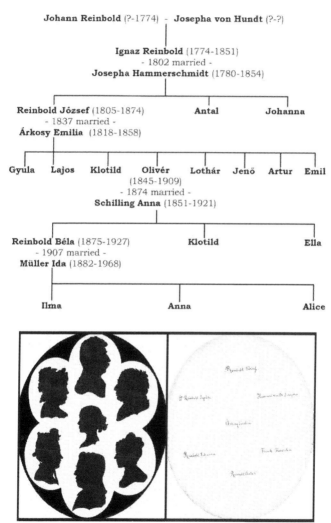

Johann Reinbold (?-1774) - Josepha von Hundt (?-?)

Ignaz Reinbold (1774-1851)
- 1802 married -
Josepha Hammerschmidt (1780-1854)

Reinbold József (1805-1874)   Antal   Johanna
- 1837 married -
Árkosy Emilia (1818-1858)

Gyula   Lajos   Klotild   Olivér   Lothár   Jenő   Artur   Emil
(1845-1909)
- 1874 married -
Schilling Anna (1851-1921)

Reinbold Béla (1875-1927)   Klotild   Ella
- 1907 married -
Müller Ida (1882-1968)

Ilma   Anna   Alice

Ignaz and the Reinbold family cc1837 contemporary
silhouette, and the back of the shadow portraits.

129

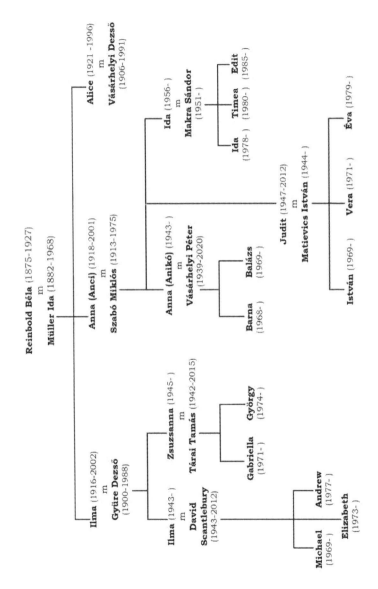

Reinbold Béla (1875-1927)
m
Müller Ida (1882-1968)

Ilma (1916-2002)
m
Gyüre Dezső (1900-1988)

Anna (Anci) (1918-2001)
m
Szabó Miklós (1913-1975)

Alice (1921-1996)
m
Vásárhelyi Dezső (1906-1991)

Ilma (1943-)
m
Dávid Scantlebury (1943-2012)

Zsuzsanna (1945-)
m
Tárai Tamás (1942-2015)

Anna (Anikó) (1943-)
m
Vásárhelyi Péter (1939-2020)

Judit (1947-2012)
m
Matievics István (1944-)

Ida (1956-)
m
Makra Sándor (1951-)

Michael (1969-)

Elizabeth (1973-)

Andrew (1977-)

Gabriella (1971-)

György (1974-)

Barna (1968-)

Balázs (1969-)

István (1969-)

Vera (1971-)

Éva (1979-)

Ida (1978-)

Timea (1980-)

Edit (1985-)

130

Ignaz's son, Josef, with daughter
Klotild, mid. 1850s.

Josef's wife, Emilia Arkosy, with her
fifth child, Lothar, cc1850s.

131

The Arkosy family, 1840s. The dress code shows the Hungarian, anti-Hapsburg feeling. Through Emilia, the Reinbold family's language changed from German to Hungarian.

The Schilling family, cc1860. Mother, Theresa Tercs is centre, the young girl in front is Anna, who later married Oliver Reinbold.

Josef's son, Oliver Reinbold, 1860s.

Mrs Oliver Reinbold, Anna Schilling, in her late twenties, 1870s.

Oliver's son, Béla, *cc*1905.

Ida, Béla's wife, *cc*1920

Dr and Mrs Dezső Gyüre, nee Ilma Reinbold, late 1980s.

Anci and Miklós Szabó with Ida, Judit and Anikó, 1958.

Alice and Dezső Vásárheyi, late 1980s. In the background: her
double self-portrait.

Another Twist in the Thermometer Story

I was idly listening to Radio 4 one day, as one does, and a programme about the folk music of the Caucasians, the Georgian people came up. The unfolding beauty, the vitality and the sheer polyphonic complexity of the voices had me spellbound. How can something as intricate, as *interwoven*, just happen? I was eager to learn from the discussion of when and how did this amazing beauty spring from. There was no answer.

All the singers knew was that their way of singing was deeply rooted in tradition, far beyond individual memory. To illustrate their point a folk tale was told. It goes like this: God was giving land to all the people on Earth to live and flourish. All the different nations were allocated a homeland, one by one, when finally the Georgians came. God was angry, 'Why didn't you come, when I called you? There is no more land left!'

The Georgians replied: 'We were singing your

praises, oh God!' and they burst into song, to show Him.

God was so deeply moved by the sounds that He said: 'There is one place left, the most beautiful place on Earth. I kept it for myself but because of your singing it will be your homeland forever.' And this is how the Georgians came to live in the Caucasus.

The story was familiar; with a thrill I realised that of course I had heard it before! In another guise it is our family's *Thermometer Story,* the one my grandfather Béla used to tell to his children, my mother told me and in turn I told my children. Strange though. I always assumed that he invented the story himself. Now I see that this can't possibly be so, he must have heard it somewhere. Could he have had a Georgian nurse maid? Unlikely. Folk stories, like songs though have 'legs', they wander from community to community, crossing country boundaries and somehow this story, in an altered form, could have arrived to Transylvania from Georgia, just like the songs Bartok collected.

In my mind there is another connection, and this is to do with inheritance from my father's side. I hardly dare to write it, it is all conjecture and please don't pick me up on it. This is not a PhD thesis, I can't prove anything, but it is just possible. You see, my maiden name is Gyüre. It isn't an entirely unknown name but neither is it very common. There is even a tiny hamlet in the north-east of Hungary, called Gyüre and all that side of the family seemed to have come from around that region.[1]

I was told that it is an Avar name. The Avars were a horse riding, semi-nomadic people. In the 5th and 6th centuries, as the Roman Empire disintegrated, they managed to conquer and rule a sizable territory, stretching from the Caucasian mountains through to the present day Romania, Transylvania and Hungary. In those turbulent times, new waves of peoples were continually arriving, coming from the East to the Carpathian Basin. Eventually the Hungarians arrived in the 9th century and the populations merged. There are plenty of archaeological reminders of Avar existence, (as there is of the Vikings in Britain). We know that they lived in round settlements, 'gyürü' still means 'ring' in Hungarian. So my name might suggest Avar ancestry. And here is my point: if words, a language, can survive 1500 years is it possible that the creation

---

[1] It seems that all the Gyüres came from a very specific and small area of Eastern Hungary. Mihály and Borbála Gyüre married in 1820 in Fényeslitke. They had four children: Mihály, Bálint, István and Hunyor. István was born 4 March 1825. He became a teacher and married Julia Benedek in 1852. László, my grandfather was born in Nagykálló in 1857. László became a Calvinist minister and took up his post in Tiszaderzs in1889 till his death in 1923.

myth of the Georgians and my grandfather's *Thermometer Story* grew from the same root, the common, but ancient Avar inheritance? For me it is a fanciful, but very pleasing possibility.

Kiskunhalas
The Kiefer Desk

1949 – 1954

This sleepy market town in the endless, all sky and sand, uninterrupted Hungarian flatlands is the scene of my childhood. In the Middle Ages it was an island, surrounded by bogs. For me Kiskunhalas was the place of all magic, of beauty and mystery.

It is in the geometrical centre of Hungary, or so we were told in school, so it follows that if it is the centre of Hungary, it must be the centre of the world and therefore the Universe. We were rather proud of this fact.

The original landscape could easily have been in Africa somewhere, somehow it does not seem to belong to the middle of Europe. The gold, loose, sparkling sand is the legacy of the Pliocene period; for nearly 3 million years, most of the Hungarian plain was a shallow, warm sea, with vast beaches.

Until the end of the 19th century, the area was

dominated by shifting sand dunes, salt pans, little lakes and isolated marshes. This created a unique habitat, with its own flora and fauna, now sadly all but disappeared. Still, here and there you can catch glimpses of it, where relentless agriculture has not caught it, maimed it, tamed it, or drained it.

But I was lucky, oh so lucky because with the neglect of agriculture and lack of manpower during and just after the Second World War, nature was able to reclaim part of what was its own. And I have seen it.

Back then, the town still had a marshy area with one raised dirt road across it. Tortoises ambled across the divide, clever little birds constructed nests by holding reeds together, I have also seen golden orioles, even a hoopoe once. Water snakes glided through the quiet waters, and frogs and toads serenaded in the evenings. And the dragonflies! We have sixty-two species in Hungary, and I think most of them congregated around our marshes. Some big and hefty, others slender, with exquisite patterns on the wings, flitting about, vivid, jewel-like as if the magic wand of an ancient wizard breathed life into his hoard of precious gems.

There were so many exciting creatures for me to marvel at, like the green scarab beetle, a pest for the roses, but so beautiful. Once a great Capricorn beetle (now a protected species) hitched a ride on a cabbage, fresh from the market and there it sat on the kitchen table, shiny, light brown, as big as the palm of my hand, with long antennae neatly folded, all the way down his side.

Of course I caught everything I could, and I was pretty good at it too, even though many of the creatures bite and sting. But I only wanted to look at them; I never, ever killed anything.

My friends were many and varied, and not only 'just' people, each equally precious. Of course there were the children from across the street and we played together most days. What this involved I have no idea; we mostly ran around and shrieked, as far as I can remember.

My best friend, however, was Mókus. We talked. We walked to school together one day, the two six-year-olds, discussing the world. She had a slight limp, the result of childhood illness. One day she was swinging a long ruler with great energy in her right hand and explained that she had a new theory: Swinging the ruler helped her to walk better. I was a bit mystified, because I could not quite see how it might. But the thought tickled me and sure enough, I admitted, it was a Theory.

During our long friendship, Mókus came up with an impressive number of new theories, (she became a humanist and went on to study applied mathematics) and her theories and ideas are still as amusing and stimulating as they ever were.

Other friends included a toad, who was as big as a saucer, living under the water butt. I used to visit him occasionally. He did not say much but nevertheless was impressive. Golden-eyed, green tree frogs called occasionally from the lilac tree, it was fun to trace the call and find the beautifully sculpted creature. Other secretive treasures lived in a ditch, just behind the pig sty. Small black toads, but they sported a vivid, bright red mottled underside. I hoped they would be poisonous as, I was told, some jungle frogs are. I never found out, but now I know that they were the European fire-bellied toads, alas on the brink of extinction.

Then there was the apricot tree. I loved his gnarled, twisted shape and the magic of fruit appearing from nowhere. He was like a benevolent old, old man, bent under the weight of his years. One spring night we had a scary, noisy thunderstorm and in the cool, thin, rain-washed grey morning found the old apricot tree broken in half. The jagged edges of the trunk stood painfully pointing skywards, the crown limp and lifeless on the ground.

I mourned that tree and, trying to come to terms with its death, I wanted to draw it.

I puzzled and puzzled. How do I show it so that I am looking at the tree, the house wall behind me and the tree in front of me? Eventually I put myself as if I was standing at the corner of the house, myself in profile, the broken tree to the right of me. Still it was not right. It bothered me greatly that it was a lie, because I wasn't standing at the corner. I was ashamed. I tore the drawing up before anyone could see it. Now I know that of course I could have chosen a different viewpoint, the tree in the foreground, me and the house in the background, but in a childish egocentric world that seemed inconceivable.

I had other secrets too, a cave underneath the lilac tree. Well, if I am truthful, it was not quite a real cave, just a small hole in the sandy garden soil, which I dug out with a spoon. I needed it to house my secret hoard. Quite by accident I found that if I rubbed a piece of brick against the taut twisted wire of our swing I could score grooves and eventually shape the brick. It took a lot of secret effort but I made two little sculptures, which, with a bit of imagination, could be construed as horses.

They lived in the cave, together with a shard of a patterned plate and my biggest treasure, a chipped marble, which I had found on the street. When I felt it was right, I went to venerate these objects and even devised a ceremony of 'Approaching the Cave'. It only lasted a summer, by the next year I had forgotten all about it. Still it was so important that now is the first time I have talked about my Cave.

The lid of a discarded shoe polish tin did not make the sanctity of the Cave, yet I stared at it often. It was green, and on it was a picture of a green shoe polish tin, with white wings. On which you could just see the picture of a green shoe polish tin, with wings. I wondered, could there be an end of ever smaller pictures of green shoe polish tins with wings? I came to the conclusion that even if I couldn't see them anymore, they could be there. It was a giddying and exciting thought, like staring into an endless cone.

We, as children had hardly any toys, apart from one or two ugly dolls, a set of dominoes and a few board games. It is interesting, though, how in a child there is an innate need to discover life's essentials, using whatever tools are at hand. I vaguely suspect that the fewer the tools, the better the understanding that develops.

So I had chanced upon the infinite variety of life forms, the possibility of death, a notion of infinity, even an inkling of the numinous.

While I was doing such great and important things, discovering the world around me, our parents settled down into the joy of everyday. Furniture was first on the list of requirements. The local carpenter, who was no Chippendale, made two beds, a table and six chairs to my father's design. Solid, heavy objects, each one. Not exactly to my mother's taste, one has to admit, East German shot putter was the simile she used. But they were, and still are serviceable.

My father still needed a desk, and one was advertised in the local plant nursery.

In the tree-covered quietness of the streets, my father and my six-year-old self walked, and chattered in pleasant agreement. Through the town, towards the station, past the monument, past the

Calvinist cemetery we walked, and into the orchard amongst the darkening trees into the glare of a single bulb of the office, to look at the desk.

The man handling the sale was helpful.

'Yes, it is from Mr Kiefer's estate. This was his own desk.'

'You know, Mr Kiefer, who produced the new pear, the Kiefer pear.'

'Very good winter variety.'

'The desk? Oh, it's made of walnut.'

'No, there is no woodworm in it.'

I liked it because the handles were in the shape of acorns. My father liked it too, because it seemed a very reliable, simple kind of desk but also because it belonged to a plantsman and a researcher; a related and honourable profession to his own, he felt. So the deal was done and henceforth the desk was referred to as the Kiefer desk in family parlance.

Only now, writing this, do I begin to wonder, what kind of pear is the Kiefer pear, since I have never knowingly eaten one? I google it, and what do I find? According to the Internet, it did not originate in Kiskunhalas at all. It was an accidental hybrid, probably a cross between the Chinese sand pear and a Bartlett. It was named in 1876 after Peter Kieffer, who found it on his Philadelphia farm and it was extensively grown in the USA in the first part of the 1900s.

Our man with the desk might have just introduced the popular American variety, and his name was not Kiefer at all.

Or he could have been someone who returned home after a trial emigration to the States, and brought the variety back to the 'old country'. This wouldn't be impossible since a million and a half Hungarians tried their luck in the States during the Depression in the 1920s.

Or could he also have been called Kiefer? A second generation of a Hungarian mother and Philadelphian father perhaps?

My father and I must have just misunderstood the story. Does it really matter? The man belonging to the desk was a gardener and he did try something new. That is good enough.

Such is the stuff of family legends.

Apricot Dumplings

The 1950s

Reading the previous pages of our life in Kiskunhalas you would be forgiven for thinking that nobody did anything but chase colourful creatures in sunny meadows, preferably with a Mozart concerto playing discreetly in the background.

The Mozart concerto had to wait till '52, when we got our first radio. It was a small, brown Bakelite box, an excellent machine; you could hear both Hungarian stations clearly and you could choose one or the other, according to your whim. Reality, with its manifold difficulties, crept into the everyday for all of us differently.

I loved my mother. I loved her, as the air I breathe, as an extension of myself and I find it difficult even now to talk about her. I thought her beautiful, that even oval face, those deep brown eyes, her dark hair. She had the grace and elegance of a Matisse portrait. Once she had a shiny, shimmery ultramarine silk dress on (they were going to visit someone) and she was breathtakingly lovely. She herself never thought so.

She tried, truly tried, and never quite believed that she succeeded. It is a pity that not enough people told her how wonderful she really was.

In an odd way from very early on, I felt older than her, almost as if she were my daughter. I thought that I understood more. I picked up on her vulnerability, because somehow she never grew out of her orphan girl status, having lost her father at twelve. She was so exposed and could be so easily wounded, that I always felt the more resilient of the two of us. All through my life I have rarely disclosed any of my own troubles, rather solved everything by myself, just to protect her from any hurt. What I did not realise at the time was that it was her who gave me the stability to be able to take on all that I did.

My parents' marriage worked wonderfully well because my father was sixteen years older, wise, loving and decisive, so she relied on his guidance. He adored her. She in turn, like a good little girl, diligently did her very best at everything, whatever the circumstances, never complaining.

Kiskunhalas in the early fifties for her was not an easy place to live.

The 'we-had-no' list by today's standards is quite shocking. No running water, it had to be carried from a public tap, several streets away. No bathroom either, only a part of the corridor curtained off at the back. No inside toilet, the wooden hut was located at the furthest part of the back garden. It was pretty scary to go out there in the pitch dark in the winter, ask any six-seven-year-old. (I was worried about wolves, obviously having heard one too many *Little Red Riding Hood* story). Electricity was still intermittent, so the paraffin light was always at the ready for the evenings. Of course no telephone, washing machine, dryer, vacuum cleaner, electric cooker, fridge, freezer, TV, or hair dryer. No ordinary human being had a car and there were no taxis either. Horse drawn carriages, the 'fiakers' lined up outside the station.

The name 'Fiaker' refers to the hackney carriage stand in the Parisian Rue de Saint Fiacre. In 1720, in Vienna, the carriages were renamed 'fiakers' (and numbered). More than 1,000 fiakers were on the road in Vienna and Budapest between 1860 and 1900. They carried on in rural Hungary well into the fifties.

And now on to a delicate subject, usually studiously avoided. It is rarely mentioned that the past is also a much smellier place than our world now. We might nostalgically recall the past, when summers were 'real' summers and winters were cold and crisp, yet the outside toilet was pungent in the heat, with sound effects from a million flies, ditto the pigsty. No daily shower in warm water for people either, a once a week heroic effort of having a bath for each member of the family was deemed to be adequate. That is when the ceremonial 'I am washing my hair' happened. Otherwise just a sponge down every morning and a quick one at night, in our case in tepid water, using two different enamel basins for your top half and another for the nether regions.

Neither could we change our outfits as freely as we do now. For a start we just did not have that many clothes. Everything had to be washed by hand and dried somewhere. So, I am afraid people, in spite of their best efforts, occasionally smelled more 'natural' than they wished to.

Living in such primitive circumstances required constant hard work. Our two rooms were fine in the summer, but winters were hard. I remember mornings when the bread had crunchy ice crystals inside the bread basket, inside the cabinet, inside the kitchen.

There was still rationing; it was my job to exchange the daily stamp for bread. Once I lost the whole book of stamps and was mortified, but with extreme luck found it on the street where I had dropped it.

Every autumn, we bought a young pig, fed it, fattened it up and the butcher came in the depth of winter to turn it into sausages, ham, cured meats, brawn, lard, crackling, to last well into the following summer. A certain percentage from every kill had to be given to the State, a much resented obligation. Apart from the odd chicken in the summer that was all the meat we had. Even the rancid fat was put to good use; from an evil smelling brew in a big cauldron in the summer, washing soap was 'cooked' from fat and caustic soda.

Oh, you kindly pigs, with your knowing little white-lashed eyes and your contented 'ruff' while we scratch you behind the ears at feeding time, forgive us.

The heaviest burden was probably carried by our mother. This once spoiled town girl, with her university degree, who spent a summer in Heidelberg as part of her education, who in her childhood was used to a live-in help, had to get accustomed to village-like surroundings and do everything herself. Two brooms, a soft for the wooden floors and a harder one for rugs, a bucket, scrubbing brush and a rag for the quarry tiles, on her hands and knees, were all the tools she had.

The twice-weekly market shopping was an ordeal. Not just because she had to carry everything back in baskets but mainly because it was expected that she should haggle.

'How much for the bunch of parsley?'

'Fifty filler.'

'Too much, look, it's limp. Give you 20.'

'How could it be, I picked it this morning. Can't do it.'

'Let it be 30.'

'OK, 30 it is.'

She had no pleasure in the game of saving a

paltry sum. It seemed shameful, because she thought that she was so much better off than the poor woman at her stall, who was up at five in the morning, lugging her precious produce, from who knows how far, and still had to look after her family.

She had no friends either, because we were newcomers in a closed, rural society and because in any case in that Stalinist age, nobody trusted anyone. Anyone could have been a communist informer.

If I think of the set-up of where we lived, it is clear that life was precarious. The State confiscated this large, originally well-to-do farmer's townhouse where we lived, near the town centre, on a leafy street. It now accommodated four families, each living in one or two rooms.

Our neighbours were a mixed bunch. The original owners were reduced to two rooms at the back, facing the farm-yard. They were embittered by their change of fortunes and resented all the people they now had to share their house with, so much so that they even refused to acknowledge a civil 'good morning.' (It was these neighbours whose whitewashed wall Zsuzsi, my sister, decorated with her large tulip drawing).

Next to them lived a young couple in one room. He was a thuggish and swaggering policeman, rumoured to be a member of the AVO, the dreaded secret police. His loud-mouthed, uneducated wife, however, was softened by her recent childbirth. The baby was called Pistike, a very nice little baby whom I was occasionally allowed to admire.

Between the young family and us, in one dark room subsisted a middle-aged couple and their flighty sixteen-year-old daughter. He was a lawyer in the town council before the war, who had been unceremoniously kicked out without a pension, as a representative of the previous regime. Due to the trauma he developed agoraphobia. The three of them lived on his wife's very meagre assistant school teacher's salary.

Then there was us.

No wonder everybody kept to themselves!

I, for my part, started school. The morning of my first day my father looked me in the eye and said: 'Whatever happens here at home, whatever is said, you must never, ever talk about it outside.' With that he took my hand and off we walked. On our way he warned me on a corner to be careful, where horses and carts might turn on their way to the market. I managed on my own after that, with a healthy fear of speeding farmers.

School learning was very easy, but the pressure at home was on.

What I did not realise up till then was that we were the wrong class. One Calvinist minister grandfather, the other one a professor of medicine, an upper middle-class mother and a doctor father did not add up as a working-class proletarian family.

A communist country, which Hungary became,

was meant to be the dictatorship of the proletariat. If your forefathers did not work in a factory, were miners or landless farm labourers, you were automatically classed as the 'enemy of the people'. The children of such families were discriminated against and only a very small percentage was deemed deserving of getting into higher education.

The spectre of his daughter not getting into university had haunted my father since I was five years old. I was told that for me it is not enough to be good, I had to be undoubtedly the best, and no praise would be due, it is my duty. While other children in my class were still on our equivalent of 'the cat sat on the mat' I was practising daily reading, aloud, with my father at home. He usually chose the lead articles of the official communist paper *Szabad Nép* (Free Citizen). He said: 'If you can read this, you can read anything.' True, I could. I can't say that I understood everything, but it didn't seem hard; it was an adventure.

Our mother meanwhile, resolutely, just carried on. And had chilblains. Her once beautiful hands became knobbly.

But she had us, her family, and she was happy. She created around us a clean, organised little world, with a clear, predictable routine, punctuated by mealtimes. If I were to be pressed to describe my childhood with just one image I would opt for us sitting round our little table in the shade, beneath the arching boughs of the giant forsythia bush, eating my mother's apricot dumplings.

Apricot Dumplings – Recipe

Ingredients:

Approx. 600g potatoes,
Approx. 300g flour
10 apricots
1 teaspoon of margarine/lard
1 egg
Breadcrumbs
Sugar

Method

1. Choose really ripe, sweet apricots. Halve them, discard stones.
2. Boil 3-4 large potatoes in their skins.
3. While cooking the potatoes, fry the fresh breadcrumbs until golden brown, and set them to one side.
4. When the potatoes are cooked and still hot: peel and finely mash.

5. Break in the whole egg, and add the fat, a pinch of salt and enough flour (about half the weight of the potatoes) to make a softish dough.
6. Roll out on a floured board, about half a centimetre thick.
7. Divide into squares; put half an apricot into each.
8. Roll into a ball, first pinching the edges together.
9. Cook them in batches in a large saucepan of gently boiling water. When the dumplings rise to the top, they are cooked.
10. Roll them in the breadcrumbs and dust with sugar.
11. Serve while still hot.

Alice, Anci, Ilma, 1926.

Ilma and Anci, going to a ball cc1936.

The bride, 1943.

Family and life in 1951, when it was a picnic. L to R: Grandmother Ida, Alice, Anikó, me, Ilma, Zsuzsi, Miklós, Judit, Anci, Dezső.

Three generations: Liz and the two Ilmas, mother and daughter 1979.

Still happy together, 1987.

Anci,
Nothing but Love

A small artificial pearl necklace, nowadays about £2.99 in a charity shop. Nevertheless, it was my first ever 'real' jewellery and my glamorous Aunt Anci, my godmother, gave it to me for my confirmation in 1954. It was the finest she could find among the meagre offerings of the state-controlled jewellery shops. The fact that I had nowhere to wear such an ostentatious treasure, did not diminish my pleasure in just having it.

My Aunt Anci, (pronounced like Nancy), the middle of the three Reinbold daughters, was a true thirties' girl. In the pre-war years she was a famous beauty, her light-blonde hair styled in the latest, face-hugging, flat waves. More than pretty, she was almost the embodiment of her age, but kind and easy-going too. She liked a lot of things: fashionable clothes, swimming, cycling, tennis, aviation and the cheerful company of handsome young men. There was no shortage of them. She was a 'jolly good sport', 'a smashing girl', and 'so dashed good looking too,' sighed the would-be suitors in their dozens.

My grandmother also became popular. Mothers of the elite of Szeged, particularly those in possession of somewhat wayward sons, discovered friendships which were never known before. Invitations followed invitations for gentle afternoon coffees, small soirees, name day celebrations, balls and dances. 'Bring your daughters too, my dear, let the young people enjoy themselves.'

And meanwhile, these other mothers thought: 'Easy to direct, nice looking, from a good family and a bit of money behind her.' Who wouldn't wish for a daughter-in-law like that? The race was on: which debonair young man about town, which calculating mother, would win the prize?

Dr Miklós Szabó was her choice, a match, it seemed, made in heaven. He also came from a distinguished intellectual background. His father was a professor of medicine, his mother one of the first female psychiatrists in Hungary. He was also a brilliant scholar. When he qualified as a doctor he had the best results in the whole country (just as my Reinbold grandfather before him) and was presented with an ornate, vellum diploma, a giant seal, and the signature of Regent Horthy. He spoke several languages, was a good chess and tarokk player, and a dazzling negotiator. (Tarokk, popular in Austria and Hungary, was an upper-class card game, the rules somewhat similar to Bridge in Britain.)

More than that, his easy manners were

accompanied by film star good looks; and even more than that, he was totally in love with her. What's to stop a couple like that living an easy and distinguished life?

The war of course.

Married in 1942, the young doctor and his bride set up their first home in the newly returned Transylvania, in Kolozsvár (Cluj). Miklós was much more aware than most people of the political nuances, the changes in rhetoric and the implications of these changes. His only sister was married to a Jew. With incredible bravery he stole chemicals from the hospital and passed them on to a friend who then created false documents for Jewish people.

No sooner had my eldest cousin, (Anikó) been born, than the Romanians took back Transylvania and they had to flee. Where was the safest place, was their question too, just like my parents. Uncle Miklós, the man with many friends in the know, led his wife and baby daughter, his own sister and mother to Budapest, and advised my grandmother and other aunt to do the same. My parents by that time were travelling towards Germany. Miklós had some justification for this decision because there was a persistent rumour that Budapest would be declared a 'safe city', like Athens and Rome, without fighting, or bombings. They reckoned the best place would be near the castle, in Buda.

We know from the history books that the city was

bitterly fought over in one of the bloodiest sieges of World War II, nowhere more so than in the Castle district of Buda. In 102 days of sheer hell, 80 per cent of the city's buildings were destroyed; all seven bridges over the Danube torn down, 38,000 civilians died of starvation, 500,000 taken as prisoners of war by the Red Army, and an orgy of violence, random executions and women raped in their thousands followed the Soviet victory.

So much for a safe city.

We have all seen the images. Unidentifiable black and grey charred buildings, desperate survivors crawling in the debris amongst nameless, faceless bodies. These are the staple of TV documentaries dealing with past or present wars, each director trying to outdo the shock of the previous ones. But they are so often repeated that we become somehow immune to it all; it becomes fiction. While we have an amalgam image of death, what we don't have is an image of life under such circumstances.

Anci wrote down her memories of the siege of Budapest much, much later and her short reminiscences help to give us some idea of their day-to-day life. In her highly selective account, she only describes random kindnesses of strangers and the 'miracles' which allowed them to stay alive but there, hidden in the unspoken, throbs the terror and bravery of existence itself.

In November 1944, in spite of the ominous German and Russian troops encircling the capital, the Hungarians still clung to the 'safe city' belief, and life in Budapest was ordinary enough. As my grandmother always liked to have handmade shoes, she and her two daughters strolled together to her shoemaker, in the heart of the city near the Margaret Bridge, enjoying the surprisingly warm autumn sunshine. Around midday an enormous blast shook the town as the beautiful bridge collapsed, taking with it trams, trucks, cars, pedestrians, horses and carts tumbling into the Danube. They could so easily have been on that bridge. Washed up swollen dead bodies littered the shore for days on end afterwards. Whether it was sabotage or the landmines, laid in preparation for a siege, or an accidental explosion, never became clear. It was a foretaste of things yet to come.

Miracle followed miracle. Miklós had to supervise the supposed train transport of hospital equipment to Hungary from Transylvania. But the train seemed to have been directed away from Hungary, towards Germany. He caught an infection and became dangerously ill as well as malnourished during the trip. Desperate, he 'jumped train' at Pannonhalma Abbey, where the monks took pity on him, fed him, and a kind German brought him to Budapest, to his wife.

Another miracle followed: Anci was able to have him immediately admitted to hospital. She visited him daily and, coming back from one of her visits, a young Hungarian soldier shouted to her from atop a lorry: 'Take it home.' and threw down a small Christmas fir tree for her to catch. She mentions with pleasure how astonished all the people on the tram were, as she carried her prize home, asking her: 'Wherever did you get the tree from?'

Miklós was well enough to join his family for Christmas Eve, at their Buda home, my grandmother and Alice joined them too, around the lit tree, celebrating together. Baby Anikó was so very pleased with the Christmas tree, said her mother. Uncle Mihály, who was living in Budapest heard a rumour: the bridges will be all blown up on Christmas Eve, so he went to Anci's to accompany my grandmother and Alice back to Pest. All the remaining bridges were blown up later on that Christmas Eve but, with incredible luck, my grandmother and Alice returned unharmed to Pest just in the nick of time.

On Christmas Day itself, the serious shooting started, it seemed safer to move to the cellar. It all worked out very well, said Anci, the baby's Moses basket was stable on top of the small coal, the sofa mattress from the apartment fitted on the larger pieces of coal, Miklós's sister found a blown-off lavatory door and made a bed on that for herself, and Miklós's mother was very happy on the reclining garden chair.

Anci made use of lulls between air raids to rush upstairs to the second floor to make pancakes for the family. Though the kitchen wasn't safe to use any more, the bathroom wood-burning water heater, with a bit of ingenuity, served just as well. At the start of the siege they could even buy fresh bread from a nearby bakery. It soon had a direct hit and shop, baker and family all perished.

There was no more food and no water. Luckily it snowed. Now they could drink and she could wash the baby's hands. More and more people crammed into the cellar from nearby ruined buildings.

'My sister-in-law and I ventured out occasionally to find some food. We saw some Russians herding a large group of women, ordering them about, and then they were all bundled into a lorry, so we hurried quickly in the other direction.' Should they have been just a few minutes earlier they too could have been caught. Those women were captured to 'service' the large army of men. It does not bear thinking about.

Someone gave them a leg of a horse. They fed on that for days.

Looting Russian soldiers came to the cellars, to the apartments, searching for gold and valuables. Anci wrote: *An older Russian saw my baby. In broken German he explained that his baby son was killed when a German soldier smashed the child to the ground. I was so very sorry for him. I could feel his grief and I just had to let him hold my daughter.*

I feel a ghastly shiver just reading about this tiny episode. Apart from the genuine compassion for a bereaved fellow parent, which Anci undoubtedly had, she had to make a quick choice. *If I let him hold my child, what if he would wish to harm her? If I don't let him hold her, would he be more likely to harm her, and all of us?* And she made the split-second decision to hand her baby over, all the while knowing that next to the baby, in her Moses basket, inside her teddy bear among the woodchip stuffing, carefully sewn in, were all the family jewels.

By February the street fighting was over, but because of the marauding Russian troops we still felt safer in the cellar. A young Hungarian man with a broken leg was lying in the cellar next to us. A Russian soldier amused himself by aiming and shooting just to the left and then to the right of his head as the injured man lay there helpless. Luckily, he was not killed and after a while there was an opportunity to take him to hospital. I hope he got well.

We were anxious now to leave Budapest and get home to Szeged. But we had to cross the only functioning bridge which was guarded by Russian soldiers. They didn't want to let anybody through. I sat on my rucksack, by the Danube, exhausted, holding the only thing of value left to us, Miklós's ornate vellum medical diploma. And suddenly I saw: There was a five-pointed star on the seal! We had never noticed it before, it was only part of the decoration, but we knew that it was of iconic significance to the Soviets. So we showed it to the guard, who obviously only read Cyrillic writing. He

170

saluted us as if we were of major importance and let us go on our way.

My grandmother, her two daughters, Anci with baby Anikó and Alice eventually arrived at Szeged only to find that my grandmother's elegant apartment had been ransacked by the Russians, although the kindly concierge had saved some bits and pieces. To cap it all an opportunistic new family, illegally but also immovably, had taken possession of the 'deserted' apartment. My long-dead grandfather's erstwhile university caretaker's family took them in and fed them for months. They were also a Transylvanian family.

Meanwhile Miklós was looking for work. My father and Uncle Miklós, in spite of their similarities, couldn't have been more different from each other. Both were doctors, good men, and clever men. Calvinists, both believed that their families were absolute priority, yet it seemed as if they had read two different books about how to live life.

Miklós, in essence, was a 'social animal'. I felt that he saw life almost as a card game, where there are winners and losers; so, he tried to guess what his opponents might think and pre-empt their moves, forged alliances, fostered his contacts and, above all, saw opportunities. He even became a member of the Communist Party.

Miklós had always been involved in events around him but he was also compassionate and daring. When my grandfather's successor, the Nobel

Prize winner Albert Szentgyörgyi, who discovered vitamin C, had to leave Hungary during the war, it was Miklós who organised the safe exit of Szentgyörgyi's two daughters by providing them (both!) with my Aunt Anci's birth certificate. (Anci went to school with one of them.) It was also Miklós who, much later in 1956, went on the dangerous mission to accompany Alice, crossing the Austrian border with her at night, and paying soldiers to turn a blind eye so that she could join her fiancé in Seattle.

Meanwhile, my father was like a steam engine, moving along on one single track. He refused to play any games and, apart from his family, he was only basically interested in how to be the best doctor and researcher he could be. Modest to a fault and intensely private, he shunned any social life and would doggedly follow his Calvinist credo of truth, simplicity and honesty. I don't think he would have recognised a business opportunity if it had hit him on the head.

Strange to think that in times of crisis the results of their actions were much the same.

Carefully considering all factors, both led their families into trouble, as opposed to away from it; both wives loyally followed; both marriages endured and became even stronger as a result of the tribulations. We all survived, in spite of their leadership. Mainly, I suspect, due to the bravery and resourcefulness of their womenfolk.

With peace, normality slowly returned. Miklós found a job in a nearby small market town, Mako, where Judit, Anikó's younger sister was born. They moved back to Szeged within a few years.

The late addition to the family, Ida, appeared in 1956. Anci dashed around on her bicycle, cooked, cleaned, made dresses, swam; entertained their friends and enjoyed their regular opera and concert visits. Something was always happening. Everything about their home was somehow more thrilling, more colourful than ours.

They had a Berger suite, with cane woven sides and large coral-coloured parakeets on the upholstery. And their espresso coffee cups were fine porcelain, turquoise and white, gold-rimmed, while ours were simple conker brown pottery.

Anci still seized on anything that was new or a novelty. They had a TV before anyone else, a modern fridge, a soda siphon, even a nylon umbrella. She welcomed Zsuzsi and me warmly, but without a fuss. We visited daily, since they shared a spacious apartment with our grandmother, and it was good to play with our cousins. Later, she received our children with equal warmth. The legacy of this is that, to this day, I can visit any of my cousins, even their children's houses, and feel at home. Her generous, warm, charismatic persona allowed everyone just to be, and bask in her presence as though in warm sunshine.

I learned a lot from my aunt.

I liked Uncle Miklós too, because he could be witty, exhilarating company, an antidote to the sober quietness in our home.

Although Alice was THE ARTIST in the family, the Reinbold inheritance – visual creativity – was also an important part of the life of the other two sisters too. When Anci spotted fabric paint (which had just appeared in shops, as a novelty) she immediately began painting the most charming Disney figures on handkerchiefs for us children.

When her first grandchildren were born, she 'sculpted' from fabric an amusing felt wall hanging, a train, where various animals look out from the carriages. She played with clay and produced a wall plaque of great beauty, depicting St George and the dragon. She embraced photography too; she was always busy, always happy.

Meanwhile Miklós was also always engaged in something, most of all perhaps in his stamp collection. He bought, sold, exchanged, corresponded, and made friendships with his many partners in Hungary and abroad. It seemed on the surface that all was well. They had three very beautiful, talented girls and materially as much as anyone could have at that time.

Yet...

Periods of silence and gloom followed Miklós's fevered activities, the intense jollity and loud laughter. At first these periods were far apart, but they became increasingly frequent and difficult to control or hide. As his moods continued their scary swings, Anci stood there, taking it all, protecting him.

I watched them once, probably in the early sixties, as they walked towards the Tisza River, away from me, in the mellow afternoon sunshine. Anci, now with the thickened waist of middle age but still elegant and tall, and Uncle Miklós tubby, balding and somehow shrunken, desperately clinging to her arm like an unseaworthy, flat river rowing boat tied to an ocean going yacht. My heart went out to them.

The depressions became more and more severe, until finally the illness won; not even the love of his family could save him. His untimely death was a terrible tragedy, which cast a long shadow over the family. Anci continued to look after her grandchildren and all seemed normal. But for us, who knew her before, it seemed as if a light had gone out of her life. She was like an amputee, hiding her secret injury. She began to distance herself emotionally and intellectually from everything around her. Gradually, gently, she glided into Alzheimer's, where nothing could hurt her any more. My two Szeged cousins looked after her at home with infinite love and patience.

She couldn't speak anymore, but when we brought her chocolates or cakes she still wanted to share all she had, and her filmy-hazy blue eyes looked at you with such gentle kindness.

Anci and Alice on the estate in Benedek with their dog, Bodri, cc1926.

Anci, ready for a themed ball, cc1935

vitéz felsőtorjai Kováts fényképészmester Szeged.

Anci and Miklós, an engagement portrait.

Miklós receiving his medical diploma
with state honours.

Miklós's parents, Prof. Med. Szabó and
Dr Gizella Kárpáti, cc1905. She was one
of the first female psychiatrists in
Hungary.

178

Miklós, Ida and Anci on holiday, *cc*1963.

The Swan Settee

Alice

I saw it and I wanted it.

There it was, in the backroom gloom of the otherwise very elegant Váci utca antique shop, the swan settee, *my* swan settee. The wooden arms curved gracefully like a swan's neck, the inlay was discreet; but it tilted precariously and the top cover was missing. The whole thing was dishevelled, just like a déclassé aristocrat who squandered away the family fortune.

I knew I was going to buy it, in spite of its broken leg.

I am sure there are images in everybody's mind, etched there forever. It does not matter how much time has passed, one moment can become eternal. I had to have the swan settee because in my mind Alice, my aunt, was sitting on it. Not on this one of course, but on another, long ago one, and in my grandmother's house.

This is going to be the story of Alice, my mother's sister. It is a love story, rivalling that of Romeo and

Juliet, but with Hungarian twists and a happy ending!

At the beginning of the 1940s, Alice was very pretty. She was also in love, as a permanent state. Just turned twenty, she was luminous like a September chestnut, with shiny dark hair, huge brown eyes, oval face and little upturned nose. Dezső Vásárhelyi was the man she wanted: the handsome, witty distant cousin. In the past, while she was still at school and he was an engineering undergraduate, sometimes he did and at other times he didn't seem to notice her. He was quick witted, secretive and flirty. She could never tell what he thought – but spent a long time mulling over the significance of his every gesture, of what he said or the way he looked at her. What started off on her part as a girlish infatuation turned into a relentless, deep, passionate longing.

When she heard that Dezső was married she was stunned, but not surprised. It had felt almost inevitable to her that she would be overlooked because she was painfully aware of her own physical disfigurement. In her early teens her spine started to curve.

Her widowed mother took her from one famous specialist to another, looking for cures. To be nearer to expert care she went to boarding school in the capital, where an endless series of remedial exercises followed, a whole year in plaster when she was fifteen, after that a hard corset with metal strips. By her late teens the damage was hardly noticeable. No more plaster, no more corsets, no more strict regimes, but all that torture left her with a lasting legacy of feeling second best where men were concerned. She compensated with a rich imaginary life and found solace in drawing and painting.

So Dezső, now a structural engineer, was married. Alice got on with her life, still living with her mother in Szeged. She got herself a degree in medical chemistry and also took lessons in fine art from a well-established local painter.

She even started to date. I remember, as a nosey three- or four-year-old, some of the 'gentleman callers'. One had a moustache, and another a most impressive pair of yellowish-brown boots which squeaked as he walked across my grandmother's shiny floor to Alice's room. I might have been impressed but neither the whiskers nor the boots did it for Alice.

Otherwise, she was just our maiden aunt. She painted, sculpted and worked in the University Hospital laboratories.

I was about four years old when she painted my portrait. 'Stop fidgeting!' was the continuous command and I truly tried but slipped up again and again. Exasperated, she said, 'If you move once more I will paint donkey's ears on you!' The inevitable did happen and I saw on the painting the hairiest, ugliest, huge, grey donkey ears growing out of my head. It was a terrible fright, I remember holding my own ears as tight as I could, trying to prevent the donkey ears growing. Strange now, thinking about it, how close a young child is to the magical thinking of our Stone Age ancestors. They painted the buffalo on the cave wall in order to have a successful hunt. Image was reality, as it felt at the time for me. I am pleased to report, though, that she painted out the donkey ears almost immediately and no lasting damage resulted.

All four cousins saw a great deal of her because we always spent the summers with my grandmother and consequently with Alice in Szeged. My mother and Aunt Anci, the two married sisters, both doted on Alice, 'the little sister'. They both tried to protect her. In their own eyes they were the lucky ones, the 'rich ones', because they were happily married and had children. 'Poor Alice,' they felt, and tried to share their riches, that is their children.

The four cousins were somehow 'guided' towards loving Alice and she in turn felt it to be her duty to help with our upbringing. Anikó and Zsuzsi readily responded; Judit and I, however, resented the feeling of manipulation and certainly did not wish to be nurtured by her. All this was just a silent mutiny, resulting in avoidance, tinged with respect, never a showy let down. We liked her well enough, but 'guided adoration' we could not do.

In any case, she heard that Dezső had got divorced, emigrated to America, and was now teaching at Seattle University.

She was hopeful again. Tentatively, timidly, she started to write to him, risking not just humiliation. In communist Hungary we were not supposed to have any connections to the West, but in her case no retributions followed; she kept her job, though the correspondence must have been regularly vetted.

And this is how I remember Alice. She sat on the swan settee, in a cloud of cigarette smoke and lavender, back against the wall, typewriter balanced on her outstretched knee, ever composing yet another letter to America.

With childlike sincerity, as if she were composing a school essay, she read out sentences, asking her mother, 'Do you think I said it right?'

I was quietly disdainful. Even as a ten-year-old I knew that you don't compose a love letter by asking your mother! But I feel chastened now because I understand more. I am sure she wasn't asking her mother's help with the 'Darling I love you and I miss the touch of your manly hands' type of sentence, she was probably just checking that she hadn't written anything politically compromising in describing our daily life.

The correspondence became life-sustaining for her and she could now say what she never managed to say face to face. As the weekly letters traversed the oceans, Dezső and Alice grew ever closer, finally announcing their engagement.

'Utter madness, of course,' was the family verdict. Everyone, apart from them, could see that it condemned both of them to a life of celibacy. It was inconceivable that communism would ever end; consequently Hungary would be imprisoned forever. The seemingly hopeless correspondence carried on, right until October 1956.

On the 23rd October something happened, even the children knew that we were experiencing 'history', the kind of stuff we learned about in school: a spontaneous, bloody revolution started against the Russian occupying forces, a hopeless, brave struggle of 10 million people against the whole might of the Soviet Union. Everyone was emotionally involved. It felt as if someone had opened a window, and suddenly fresh, clean air surged through the whole country. Only now did people dare to say openly how much they hated the regime. Hope was in that air, and, for a brief second, it seemed that we might get away with it. The western borders were opened, if people wanted to leave, they could.

The whole family started to say to Alice: 'Now is your chance. GO!' She was timid, though, and kept waiting for what tomorrow might bring. Well, it did not bring much good.

The revolution did not go as well as we had hoped, the Russians were defeating us. The state radio in an endless loop only broadcasted the national anthem, interspersed with desperate pleas to the West: HELP US! No outside help had come. The borders were being closed down again.

My Aunt Anci's husband, Uncle Miklós, was the hero of the hour. With no small risks to himself he offered to take Alice across the border to Austria. I remember her last night at home. Anci was bathing baby Ida, trying to be calm, but the tension was palpable, although we children were not told what was about to happen. Within a few days Uncle Miklós was back in Szeged. He managed it by bribing a farmer and crossing the border at night.

We soon heard that Alice had arrived in a refugee camp in Klagenfurt, and had managed to contact Dezső.

The rest of the story is rather wonderful. Dezső immediately sent her an aeroplane ticket and they were married in Seattle. For another forty years, until Dezső's death, they lived in great harmony and contentment in Seattle. Alice would have liked children but a cancer scare put a stop to that. Instead, she painted and sketched and had exhibitions, while Dezső steadily climbed the academic ladder and became a well-respected professor.

The political climate had changed in Hungary too: travel in and out of the country became easier. The wrench when Alice left Hungary on that dark December day turned out to be not as final as everyone feared. Their yearly visit to Hungary certainly caused a stir in the family. In a frenzy of friendly rivalry, my mother and Aunt Anci were trying to outdo each other, who could cook them the nicest meal? Who could think of a programme which they would enjoy?

Alice and Dezső accepted this homage with great civility, reciprocating with American trinkets (unusable leather purses and key rings and Indian beadwork) and never stayed in anyone's house, but always in a hotel.

The blue airmail letters again criss-crossed oceans and continents. She talked about their trips, about the squirrels in her garden, about their friends, who were incidentally all Hungarian, and sent pictures of all her paintings. She 'twittered' like a bird, not much philosophy, no deep meanings, no malice, no irony. Frankly, I thought her writing a bit dull. But they were precious for the sisters and her mother. The whole family gathered for each letter to be read aloud, no secrets were ever possible.

Alice died two years after Dezső. She fell asleep in an armchair, her sewing still in her hand, getting ready for her next trip home to Szeged.

She was the most contented person I have ever known, obviously very happy in her marriage.

Her paintings, though, talk about something else. The one in my flat, a present to my parents, is of driftwood: the trunk of an ancient, giant sequoia, bleached by many summers, battered by wild Pacific Ocean waves, broken, lying on featureless bare sand; its lifeless ghostly branches grope blindly into an empty blue sky. All her work is compelling, none are easy to interpret, but most are filled with a nameless longing.

Anikó and I, the two eldest nieces, went to clear her house. We unearthed about fifty kilos of shiny, tangled, tinkling costume jewellery, forgotten, worthless. It was shocking to chance upon yet another bundle. They turned up everywhere, amongst the cutlery, in shoeboxes, in her sewing baskets, in drawers, in the loft. Yet she dressed so soberly! It was an unexpected façade to the existence of my timid, warbling, birdlike little aunt and her doctor, professor husband!

Can you ever assume that you know anybody?

Anikó and I also brought their ashes home, because the sisters could not bear the idea of them resting in a foreign land, so far away. We also packed up and brought back Alice's paintings.

Their ashes rest together with my parents in the Szeged Calvinist cemetery. ('Ha!' my mum will say, 'at last, at last, they are staying with me!')

And the paintings?

Well, as it turns out, she was a significant artist and her oeuvre is greatly admired.

Alice as a child, *cc*1923.

The young artist, *cc*1940.

The American Dream, 1950s. A photo Dezső sent to his sweetheart back in Hungary.

Once Sweethearts In Hungary

Professor, Refugee Bride Meet Press

Finally married in Seattle, 1957.

Alice's first visit from Seattle, 1958.

In Seattle, 1988, just after my father's death. This photo explains more of the sisters' relationship than any words can do. In the background is Alice's studio.

Mamika, Our Dear Grandmother

Think of a beautiful tree, like a mature weeping willow. You see it at a distance, graceful, venerable, the old trunk full of twists. The tender branches nearly touch the ground as they wave gently in the breeze. Come nearer, you see the knotty bark, the individual younger branches, you see each leaf. Come even nearer, you touch the old trunk; you are enclosed in the welcoming green igloo of gentle, swaying shoots. Seeing switches to feeling. Only tiny details remain visible, not the whole.

Only when I thought I had finished writing, having said all I wanted to say, did it occur to me that I haven't honoured my Grandmother Ida with a section all of her own. If I really didn't like her or I didn't know her I could possibly shrug my shoulders and extricate myself from the unseemly omission but that's not the case at all.

Sometimes you can be too close to someone to describe them accurately, they become a feeling, and they are part of you. That is how it is with our Grandmother Ida. She was so deeply rooted in our lives that she became almost invisible. Still, I will try to give some sort of account of her, just impressions and snippets, a tone of voice, her 'colour'.

We were taught to call her Nagymami, and in the diminutive, 'endearing' form Nagymamika, which got simplified to Mamika. From Grand Mum to Little Mum. We all adored her.

In early life she was strikingly lovely. It wasn't the pouting, simpering kind of beauty, much more the Ingrid Bergman type: tall, even featured, with dark hair and lively blue eyes. We knew her as a white-haired old lady, with a bent back, always in mourning, wearing black or grey. She was stylish and dressed with care, though with the minimum of adornment, just a broach or a pair of earrings. But her eyes forever retained the sweet clarity of youth.

Even now, we, the granddaughters, still repeat to each other with a giggle, feeling harassed and less than immaculate: 'You remember what Nagymami said? You only have to make sure that your hair is perfect and your shoes are polished, what goes in-between, if it is clean, it will not be noticed.'

Her life's major events can be summed up in just a few sentences. She married Doctor Béla Reinbold in her native Transylvania. They had two children but tragically both died of scarlet fever. They went on to have three more girls, moved to Szeged when the University of Kolozsvár was re-established in

193

Hungary. Her husband died heartbreakingly early in Szeged. Here she remained though, bringing up her daughters alone. Later, as we all lived in Szeged, she helped with our upbringing too.

It was quite a journey she made, in more ways than one, to become our kindly and wise guardian. Born in 1882, the youngest girl of five siblings, she started life in a financially stable, affectionate home in Transylvania. It was the golden age of the last decades of the 19th century. On the surface everything seemed prosperous, peaceful and predictable. Nothing indicated that her life would be any different from those of her forefathers.

She finished school at sixteen, which, in those days, was deemed enough academic learning for a girl, even in the most affluent families. Her parents sent her for a lengthy stay with not quite high aristocratic but still 'upper crust' relatives in Vienna, to complete her education. This was the Vienna of corsets, long dresses, imperial splendour, waltzes, balls, elegant soirees and refined conversation, where social protocol was strictly adhered to. Not to know which the peach knife is, or when and to whom do you present your hand to be kissed meant 'Provincial', a terrible shame.

Whatever I know of 'gracious entertaining' I have learned from her, mainly from name day celebrations. It is a European custom, somewhat equivalent to the English birthday parties but has two great advantages. First of all, the names are in the calendar, so anyone who knows your name, also knows when to congratulate you. And the other good thing about it is that you don't have to declare just how many name days you already have under your belt.

These name day events, hers and her friends', regularly punctuated life. They were the glue which held her tightly knit little group, mainly ex-Transylvanian families, together. Baking started days before, dainty crescents of walnut shortbreads, Linzer torte slices, cheese twists. The table was set with the delicate, 'best' china, and the tiny liqueur glasses were gleaming on the white, finely worked tablecloth.

The best thing for us was that the children were also part of it all; we could sit in and help to offer cakes or be just plain nosy. The guests brought flowers. Even now, the heady scent of tuberose or the sight of flowering amaryllis immediately take me back to those Ida Days.

Another, unmissable yearly event was the spring visit to the old magnolia tree. It was, and still is, the jewel of the stately park in the centre of Szeged town. The stunning beauty of those huge, pink, tulip-like flowers gave her enormous pleasure.

Mamika's sanctuary, by the time we knew her, was just one room in Aunt Anci's spacious apartment. Here she slept at night or just withdrew in the afternoons, and here she entertained her friends. She was separate yet part of the family; a usual kind of arrangement at the time, and worked very well. All her granddaughters saw her daily.

I was there one evening when she tried to get out of an armchair. Standing up she just fluttered to the ground, silently, like a falling leaf. Her femur broke. Nowadays perhaps a hip replacement would solve the problem, but it wasn't available in the early 1960s. She lived like this, with her broken bone, being moved from wheelchair to bed, to wheelchair again for another four years. When the pain became too much to bear there was only morphine.

It must have been excruciating for her but only once did I hear her say that she was waiting for the time when she would meet her long-dead husband and children. Selfishly, we wished to keep her with us. But that was the end and she was contented, even in those last four difficult years. How she achieved that, defies understanding.

Is there anything I can say about my grandmother Ida which makes her any different from any other loving grandmother? She cooked and she baked. Light as a feather sweet yeast buns (arany galuska), the supermarket 'tear and share' brioches are but a pale imitation of the real thing, warm, straight out of the oven, baked in a round tin, turned out as a mound and served with hot white wine custard. Or the mystic 'vizenkullogo' (an untranslatable name, it means something like 'water plodder'). It is yeast dough, wrapped in a greased cloth napkin, placed in water and as it proves it slowly wobbles, turns and rises to the top.

Her button box was full of curious, shiny treasures. She cuddled us, if we needed it, and everything we wanted to tell her she found interesting. She had such a lively mind, conversation was never dull, whatever the topic. Her favourite reading was *Life and Science*, an ambitious but entertaining weekly. She was indeed another mother, but with a difference. None of us needed to achieve anything, give anything in return, we were accepted and loved simply because we existed. There is no greater gift you can give to anyone.

I only remember just one occasion being told off. I would have been around eight years old. It was a hot summer day, the door wide open to the balcony. She was preparing lunch. We decided that the balcony needed to be washed. So four of us started to carry water in makeshift containers from the tap, through the kitchen, past the cooker, through the door, liberally splashing it everywhere en route. We were busy and very contented. Meanwhile she was trying to cook. Suddenly she said, 'Children, either in or out!' We were shocked and stopped immediately. Such harsh words from our grandmother! If it was me in a similar situation I would have shrieked in exasperation but her quiet 'either in or out' was effective enough to stay with me for a lifetime.

Her stories of events a long time ago, were gentle too, just on the edge of funny. They gave us a glimpse of a fading world, now only visible to her. We liked to hear stories about the childhood of our mothers. 'Tell us the story about the summer house,' we begged and she started in her soft, Transylvanian accent.

'You know, I had already told you that we used to go home to Transylvania and spend the whole summer in Benedek. Aunt Ella and Aunt Klotild, my sister and sister-in-law ran the estates all year round, but in the summer the whole wider family gathered here, with all their children. It was a cheerful time for everyone. Once though one of my children, I don't remember now which one, became feverish. Just in case it was something contagious I nursed her in the summer house, well away from the others.'

We imagined this happy place, the spacious house, the summer house and the brook at the bottom of the large garden, beyond the orchard. It sounded great fun to have so many cousins about.

'One night I woke to the sound of noisy footsteps around the house, to ominous, heavy breathing, and crushing broken branches.

'Bandits! I thought, because there were always scary stories of rough gangs coming down from the high mountains to rob defenceless people.

'I was petrified. I am all alone, we will be murdered because the main house is too far away for anyone to help us. There I crouched in the darkness, hardly daring to breathe. Better not make any noise, I thought, better not light the paraffin lamp. I quaked and prayed and at last the noises ceased. We were spared, I thought.

'Dawn came, I rushed to the main house and everyone came to investigate. No sign of bandits but all around the summerhouse the grass was chewed and trampled down. It was clear that a neighbour's buffalo herd escaped from its regular pasture and decided that the well-kept garden was a much better place to have a midnight snack. We could laugh at my groundless fright.'

We wanted to know what a buffalo was like, we have never seen one. And how come they were there?

'Oh, they are large, black beasts, with big horns and a hump, but their milk is wonderfully rich. You know, they still keep buffalos in Transylvania just as in Italy.'

We listened and shivered with terror as she told the story. But we knew the ending, so it wasn't really bad. This often told story reminds me of the wise English saying: 'Today is the tomorrow we worried about yesterday. And all is well.' Meaning that our greatest fears often turn out to be groundless – ALL IS WELL! While amusing us, she was also teaching us.

Everything around her was special, different and magical. Her room was a sitting/living room. One low single bed in a corner, in the daytime covered with a rough, dark grey, hand-woven blanket and a range of cushions leaning against the Persian carpet wall hanging. Lots of pictures, scenes from Transylvania, sepia photographs in lovely oval frames, the swan settee, a low, round inlaid table and low-backed, curved armchairs around it. All old, all family pieces from Transylvania. Harmonious, understated, calm, welcoming.

She was almost invisible, because she was the welcoming, embracing shade of the ancient tree and she was the quiet peace, where 'all is well.'

But how? How can a human being achieve such serenity, such crystal clear perfect loving, to understand all and forgive all? A question I never asked at the time, while she was alive.

In my mind I went back, visited her again in her room and looked around. There by the low divan bed was a copy of *Life and Science*, the needlepoint cushions in a neat row, the old family furniture, oval-framed, faded sepia photographs of her parents above her bed, and a few En Plein Air landscape paintings of Transylvania decorating the white walls. Art history to us now, but just think that these vibrant images, when they were purchased, were the latest thing!

Like a time detective, I searched. And there was my clue in the shape of a small, square painting, quite a skilled copy of a Murillo cherub, a canvas, without a frame. We were told that she herself painted it but it added an odd note to the otherwise harmonious room, for several reasons. The topic itself was surprising. You will never find religious imagery in a Calvinist home, however beautiful they might be. No saints, angels, no Mary, no Jesus with a bleeding heart, no statuettes, no crosses. A cherub is an 'inbetweeny', a kind of nameless baby angel, so I suppose it doesn't count, but still it was the only such 'churchy' image of my childhood.

Clue number two, that there is more going on here than meets the eye. (Or put better, doesn't meet the eye!) It hung high up, right near the ceiling, in a corner, so it was hardly visible. I was told it was there to hide a chimney hole in the wall for a wood burner stove, which she did not have. Why put a painting there, when a white piece of cardboard, painted the same colour as the wall would have been less obtrusive? And why no frame? It was out of character, because everything was so finished and neat in her room. She painted it herself, we were told. Nobody said when this might have been. It could easily have been before she got married because young ladies did paint, there was nothing surprising about that. Maybe she was shyly proud of her early painterly efforts, but in her mind it did not merit a frame or to be displayed amongst the 'good' professional paintings.

There could be much more than an early exercise in painting. She was raised Calvinist but her husband was a Catholic, like all Reinbolds since

Ignaz. She embraced her husband's faith seamlessly. It is the same God, she argued, you just talk to him differently in another church and she liked the candles and why St Anthony in particular, we'll never know. The very Catholic image of the cherub, displayed almost 'accidentally' and hidden in plain sight, was a quiet assertion of her private beliefs. It would have given her some inner strength.

I tried to identify the Murillo work and my heart skipped a beat when I found the one I think she copied. It is *Cherubs Ascending to Heaven*. Oh dear God!

Now I realise that the only place anyone could look easily at the cherub was from her bed, lying down. It was put there deliberately so that she could still say of an evening, 'Goodnight, children, sleep tight,' to Edith and Josef, to those long dead children.

I think she was loved so much because she found a path which led to contentment. How cathartic events are experienced, and what actions they lead to later on in life vary from individual to individual. She carried so much pain. But her pain was private. She had lost her homeland, lost two children, lost her husband, and later even lost a lot of her cherished possessions. The erstwhile wealth was all gone. About possessions she never talked again. But her ties remained strong to her family, back in Transylvania; emotionally she never left them. How could we children understand her endless ache for her lost homeland, when we thought that Szeged was perfection itself? We could not understand it, but we felt it. I did not get it then.

I do now.

I think I might have accidentally stumbled upon her private solution of how to reach out to her lost children. About her husband, I don't know. The connection must have been there, but the ache was too private, too well camouflaged and too hidden. Let it remain so.

But the result of all these losses was that she loved and appreciated us, the alive ones, without reserve. Having stood at the 'edge of the void' she realised that existence is not assured, that everything and everybody can be taken away from you. So everything she did have, became infinitely precious.

Who loved her most? Which one of the five granddaughters? Could it be Judit, who helped to look after her physical needs in those last tough years, though she found the task difficult? Or Zsuzsi, who trusted the grandmother's love more than anybody else's? Perhaps Little Ida, that sparkling light of a child, who was the constant, devoted companion of the bedridden invalid. Maybe Anikó or myself, because we are the oldest, and feel that we knew her best? This is a silent, never discussed question because we all believe it is ourselves. But we never asked whom did she love most, because we knew that her love was infinite, therefore equal.

Every single item which was hers and now is in one of the granddaughter's homes is treasured. When we visit each other we touch the green vase, the ornate fruit stand or whatever and quietly say: This was Mamika's. And the owner says: Yes.

We still make a pilgrimage to the magnolia tree when it is in full bloom and say to each other: Do you remember?

They say that there are subterranean rivers on the Yucatan peninsula, with crystal clear waters. Though the surface is arid, tree roots are able to reach down to the unfathomable deep. Plants, animals and humans alike are all richly sustained by the unseen source. Her love was like those clear waters.

That is how I imagine ancestor worship.

Ida as a young girl, cc1895.

Ida's parents, Mihály Müller and
Ida Kristyóri, 1870s.

Ida Kristyóri centre, with friends,
before her marriage, 1860s.

205

With husband Béla, *cc*1905.

In the park where the magnolias bloom, with granddaughter Ida, *cc*1962.

Friendships survive. With Mrs Bucsi, widow of another professor from Transylvania, cc1958.

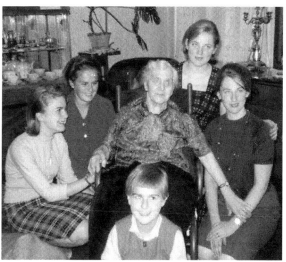

The five granddaughters. Little Ida in front, L to R: Judit, Anikó, Zsuzsi, Ilma, 1965.

Water Plodder

Ingredients:

500g plain flour
170g lard
1 sachet dried yeast
100ml milk, + spoonful of sugar
3 egg yolks
250g sour cream
Caster sugar to dust

Method:

1. Activate the yeast in lukewarm milk and a spoonful of sugar.
2. Melt the lard.
3. Beat the egg yolk with the liquid lard until it is thick.
4. Add the flour, activated yeast and enough sour cream to form a stiff dough.
5. Knead this dough well until it is smooth and elastic.

6. Grease a large tea towel with lard, and place the dough in the centre. Tie the opposite ends, very loosely, to form a bundle. Slide a wooden spoon through this knot.
7. Fill a large pan with cold water and submerge the bundle in the water, with the wooden spoon holding the knot above the water. The dough will sink, but in an hour or so, as it proves, it will start to wobble and slowly 'plod' to the surface.
8. Turn it out on to a sugared and floured surface, pat it out into a 1 cm thick rectangle and cut it into longish strips. Fold the strips in half and twist 2 strands together.
9. Prove again and bake at 180°C, for 18-20 min. When it's ready it should be golden and the sugar slightly caramelised.

Learning about Life

1950s

I experimentally painted my nails with nail varnish once. Red it was, a lovely colour, I thought. My father noticed it. 'What do you think you are doing?'

'Just want to be pretty,' I said meekly.

'Take it off at once,' he ordered. And as an irrefutable argument he added: 'When I was travelling in Italy before the war, prostitutes standing on street corners had painted nails!'

I wasn't even sure that I knew what a prostitute was. Without a word, I wiped it off (and carried the hurt).

Going to an academically excellent but all-female girls' school, having a sister and three girl cousins, and no outside social life, temptations were thin on the ground.

I would have been around fourteen when a boy asked me to go to the cinema with him.

'You are not going,' said my father. No explanation given, just that one sentence. I didn't argue, protest or sneak out. I didn't go. I just stood by the window looking out, longing to get away, and I was so, so sad.

My dear father, he was so concerned for his daughter's morality. Frugality and finding self-adornment morally abhorrent were jumbled up in his mind as one concept; for his daughters this meant a tricky navigation between Scylla and Charybdis. Fortunately, our mother was a quiet but steadfast ally. Being teenagers and connecting home life with that of the world around us, realising that there were such things as boys even, was complex for both my sister and me, but we managed. Eventually we found our place in the universe.

Where I got to, might be best illustrated by an ancient folk tale and my poem, based on the story. What is in a folk tale? Told and re-told over millennia, it transcends boundaries of time and space, giving pleasure each time it is repeated. It also acquires a form as perfect, pure and as shiny as a pebble on the beach, washed, tumbled, awkward corners smoothed away by the relentlessly crashing waves. It contains truths, a meaning way beyond the surface story, forever valid for all mankind. Jung knew that, so did Clarissa Estes, so did Bartok, Vaughan Williams and the Aborigine storytellers. I count myself incredibly lucky that in the highly censored 1950s, when I began reading, the literary diet for children was mainly our own and other nations' stories. This is one way our ancestors reach out to us and through gentle entertainment they teach us how to be, how to be human, where our boundaries are.

This is a re-telling, it isn't my invention. Only the words and the poem are mine. I am dedicating it to all my female relatives, up and down the generations, who for the most part have chosen well...

The Woodcutter

Once upon a time, a long time ago, the woodcutter was walking home through the dark forest, tired and hungry after a long day's work. He was longing for the comforts of home, his cheery wife by the fireside and a good dinner. But first he had to go through She Wolf Country. He thought he caught a glimpse of her, though was not sure. He aimed and shot. When he arrived home he found his dead wife slumped lifeless in a pool of blood by the half-cooked dinner, the fire still smouldering.

As it is told we see events from the woodcutter's, from the male's point of view. But here is another story too, but hidden, that is hers. I wrote, what I feel it is telling me, in a poem form.

The Song of the She Wolf

Beware, beware,
For we are the connection
We are the beginning and we are the end

Kill us and we bleed
And we are nothing
But we rise and rise again
You can't kill us

We are your creation
We are your creator,
We are loyalty and we are strength

We are the sun and the moon
We are the pulse
Seek to tame us and you stifle yourself

We are, we are, we are
Each one of us,
Seek the She- and find the wolf

Oh the vanity of man, Proud Provider
Subdue, rule, and tame the wolf
Make us into sweet little yapping doggies

Yet
Again and again,
While we have breath, even subdued,
We are wild

You think force is the way
To tame, to scare, to eradicate?
Love us well instead.

One quick fumble
Is not enough to say
'I'll never forget What's-Her-Name'
Not enough.
What's-Her-Name you can never forget,
For how could you forget whom you had never
known?

Love us well. Don't be frightened. Dissolve in us.
We are your future and we are your past.
You can kill but you cannot tame.
Kill us and you have killed your very self
And whimper alone in the moonlight.
Love us well. And may you live.

In life some of us make quite a journey. We might not end up where we thought we would when we were young.

This is a holiday photo from 1950. L to R: Zsuzsi, Grandmother Ida, Mother and myself. You'll understand what I mean about 'journey' when you look at the following two pictures of the grownups when they were younger.

Our grandmother changed from an elegant Victorian society beauty to this elderly lady with bent back, worn clothes and much mended, shabby shoes with socks.

Our mother, the stylish '40s bride, emerges ten years later in a dress she made herself, with a bag which is strictly utilitarian; nobody could accuse it of being chic! Zsuzsi and I are wearing one of the three summer dresses we possessed and our only, alas unmatching, cardigan. I love this picture because it is so true. It was like that.

I love the picture for another, art historical reason too. In communism, art, as every other aspect of life was regulated. The dictum was that art must serve the regime. They called it Socialist Realism. It was declared that since communism is the dictatorship of the proletariat, all art forms must clearly praise the working man. There were an awful lot of canvases depicting strong, muscular men in various industrial settings, and brave women, looking heroically into the future, surrounded by an assortment of machines. Some of these paintings are very good but it was a monotonous diet.

What I find so funny is that our mother's stance and her expression is precisely how the brave proletarian women were depicted.

Indeed she was strong and defiant, a true heroine. Bravery is not the privilege of just one class of people. Whatever Mother and Grandmother were before, they battled on, neither of them gave up. And we all cling together. We, the children are learning about life.

Think of the journey our grandmother, Ida, (on the left) made from this young lady in 1899 to the 1950s. Just ten years before the 1950s photo on page 215, my mother looked like this.

Goldfish and Mickey Mouse

The Cold War

1958

On the bookshelf, in front of Tolstoy's memoirs and Nansen's journey, stands an ornament of a cheap porcelain fish, washed out knicker-pink in colour. Gold squiggles add insult to injury on its poor curved body and around its gaping mouth. Not a maker's mark anywhere, not a number, it does not do anything, it just gapes. It can't be used for anything, not flowers, nor sugar or pencils. Its whole purpose is gaping in hideousness.

Heavens, I hear you cry, in the style of a P. G. Wodehouse hero, have the Gyüres taken leave of their aesthetic senses? Well, yes, but let's be charitable and say they have suspended their artistic judgement, just for once. But hear me out as to why.

It happened like this:

By 1958, Hungarian relationships were less frightening to the mighty Soviet Union. Of course the Soviet troops were still stationed on Hungarian soil but they behaved less aggressively. My father was at that time the head of the local infectious diseases hospital and one day a Russian patient, the wife of an officer from the local barracks, was admitted. This would never have happened before 1956.

There was, and still is a shameful custom in Hungary, the so called 'gratitude money'. Doctors' state salaries are so low that they usually gladly accept payment from grateful or intending to be grateful patients. Now as it happened, my father never, ever accepted any money, as a matter of principle. He just treated everyone to the utmost of his capabilities. When he retired, he even got a personal letter from the then Minister of Health, declaring that he was the only doctor in Hungary who had refused, what amounts to, bribery. No doubt, the custom was the same in Russian circles.

Thankful for genuine kindness and desperate to reciprocate, the Russian family arrived with a foot-tall bottle of the most sickly-sweet scent, in the shape of the Kremlin, and a fish ornament. To refuse the Kremlin, whatever it contained, would have been unthinkable, nevertheless in the bin it went, as soon as it got home. However, the fish stayed. Because it was given with good will, with honesty. They gave what they had, their Russianness. You see, this would-be-golden fish is a symbol, a reference to a Russian folk tale and the subject of a famous Pushkin poem.

This is the story:

An old and very poor fisherman catches a talking golden fish. The fish asks to be returned to the sea but promises to fulfil the old man's wishes. He asks nothing for himself, but his greedy wife wants and gets ever greater things: more bread, a new washtub, a bigger house, servants and eventually fabulous wealth. But the fish disappears, never to be seen again when she finally asks to be the ruler of all seas, and the old man and his old wife are back in their ramshackle hut, poor and hungry.

What is this golden fish? Read it again! Sounds vaguely familiar? Man wanting more and more from nature? Exhausting all resources, growing richer, lazy and arrogant, wanting even more, imagining that he can command nature itself. Where does he end up? Destitute and hungry.

In our 21st century existence in the time of deforestation, habitat loss, climate change, irreversible pollution of land, oceans, even outer space, the story is as timely a warning for us now, as it could ever have been. But how did those simple farmers know this, centuries and centuries ago?

Mickey Mouse

Round about the same time as we received the ugly ornament there were other presents too from my Aunt Alice, who by then lived in Seattle. Like most émigré Hungarians, she sent a large parcel every year to the 'old country'. Eagerly anticipated by all females of the family, these parcels usually contained fabric remnants and other bits and pieces. These were greatly appreciated because until the mid-sixties, dress materials were of a very bad quality and the choice limited; wearable readymade clothes from shops hardly existed.

From the 1957 parcel I got a length of yellow thickish Crimplene, a very new, easily washable synthetic stuff, and a navy-blue cotton blouse material. I knew what I wanted; I had seen it in *Burda*, the West German fashion magazine with tailoring patterns. This was the height of sophistication for us, full of 'real' Western ideas which we could copy and so feel part of a wider world. These magazines were precious, studied eagerly, and passed from hand to hand.

So, my dear mother made the ensemble for me. There I was, mousy blond, not too slim, piercingly pale complexion, which tended to get blotchy, in this canary yellow pinafore dress, looking paler, squarer, more awkward than ever in my life, nothing like the cool, tanned *Burda* model, and to top it all, in that outfit, there was nowhere to hide.

Unmitigated disaster though the dress was, I was given something else too. A real Mickey Mouse figure! It was a love affair at the first sight. I took him to school with me; he sat on my desk where I could gaze at him unhindered by the French Revolution, the circumference of a circle, or the finer points of a heroic poem. Just bigger than my hand, he had big, longing yet smiling eyes, always on me, the arms and legs were warm to the touch, smooth, firm but not hard, and he smelled so sweet, clean and enticing.

For three days he came to school with me, but the enchantment broke as suddenly as it had occurred and I never looked at it again.

I wondered much later, what this power was, which had me so strongly in its grip? I understand it now. Those big eyes, the disproportionately big head, the touch of the limbs and mainly the smell awoke, in my thirteen-year-old self, a nascent maternal urge, powerful, unexplored. And since it was not a baby and it could not respond, it was discarded.

What incredible sophistication, what knowledge of psychology is needed to design the precise shape of eyes, the proportion of the head, the right combination of fleshy tones and primary colours. Most of all to imbue the whole figure with the correct, evocative scent, calling on our earliest, deepest senses in order to manipulate such elemental emotions! How many creative people, how many experts contributed to its making?

I still get uneasy whenever I see the TV advertisements of happy families, excited at the prospect of going to Disneyland. The story line usually involves the 'no, we can't afford the trip,' the 'yes, children, we have saved and we shall go,' and ends up with an ecstatic child being embraced by a giant Mickey Mouse, exhausted but contented parents looking on, safe in the knowledge that they have ensured all future happiness for their offspring.

So goes the ad.

Do we really want to pay for our children to be embraced by a half-human, half-monster giant? Nevertheless, the enchantment, like the wicked fairy's curse, works. We flock willingly to part with our cash. In the hope of what?

With the two presents, the fish and Mickey Mouse, two ideologies crashed in our innocent household, the cold war was fought in miniature and neither of them won!

The fight is still on: human values versus corporate greed and mass manipulation.

I wish I had kept the Mickey Mouse figure, though; it could have been sold for good money on e-Bay.

The Calvinist College at Mezőtúr

Without doubt the determining factor in my father's life, affecting education, morality, belief system, even personal relationships, was the eight years he spent at Mezőtúr.

It puzzled me how a college like this can seemingly spring out of nothing, exist for 400 years unchanging in its spirit, and inspire such loyalty. Mezőtúr is a small town, by a brook in the middle of the featureless Hungarian plane. Even now it only has 9,000 inhabitants.

Yet this is where it is, this is the place where the famous school was established in 1530 which had such an undeletable impression on my father and on the many generations before and after him.

The college was academically highly ambitious and open to influences from abroad from the start. By 1558 a dozen of Mezőtúr's old boys were studying at Wittenberg and six at Krakow University, bringing back new ideas to their old school. From the start the language used in teaching was always Hungarian, not Latin.

My father described the style of teaching in his

time as unaffected, natural, and wide ranging. As a highlight he remembered translating Virgil, almost as a game, to find the most beautiful, most appropriate Hungarian phrases for the Latin original. He loved mathematics as well as literature. The pupils were taken on trips to Vienna, and to the Carpathian Mountains. If the teachers saw a talent in someone, they fostered it, and quietly helped needy pupils financially, by finding bursaries or tutoring jobs.

However, the spirit of engaging with the students is even more remarkable. As early as 1795 in its 'Duties of Teachers' it stipulates that a teacher must never speak angrily to a pupil, even if it is deserved, let alone shame them or swear at them. The only acceptable retribution for wrong doing is calm speech, explaining what the pupil has done wrong, and what the consequences are. Students were welcomed from all backgrounds, regardless of religion.

All this sounds totally familiar to us today. No corporal punishment, a respect for the individual, persuasion as opposed to prohibition and religious tolerance. But we are not talking about the 21st century; these principles governed the school for 300 years!

The college also had an extensive library and up-to-date scientific instruments for demonstrations, slowly accumulated over the centuries. Tradition dictated the accepted duty of every old Mezőtúr student. When they finished their studies at home and continued abroad they brought back books. These would be printed or laboriously hand copied.

The same applied to instruments. He brought back the latest technology, the latest ideas. These young men often also stayed on to teach for a few years after their foreign studies. This helped them to find their feet and also ensured a continuous influx of new ideas. I find this continuous recycling, regenerating self-sufficiency, the 'everything on a shoe-string' mentality deeply touching. And it produced men like my father.

How a college like the one in Mezőtúr could develop the way it has, has its roots in European politics, religion and scientific thought. It is in essence very different from the English path. A nation, like Hungary, at the crossroads of Europe, would always want to be informed of what's happening in the world. It is a matter of safety and keeping up with the neighbours. An island nation, however, would say: we ARE the world.

The other great difference of course is Henry VIII's decisive separation from the Catholic Church. The three timelines, the Science Revolution of the 16th and 17th century, the history of the Reformation and landmarks of Hungarian history of the period explain the paths, and puts the school into its historical context.

Incidentally, understanding the significance of these events will go a long way towards making sense of much of subsequent Hungarian history, even some present-day attitudes. The Scientific Revolution which was kick-started in 1543 by Copernicus's heliocentric theory was followed by innumerable new discoveries and inventions of new tools. Amongst others, Kepler's laws of planetary motion, Galileo's theories of motion and inertia and Newton's discovery of the laws of gravitation led to a massive shift in the Judo-Christian understanding of the world. People started to believe that while God created the universe, through science it is possible to understand the mechanics of the universe.

The 18th century intellectual movement, the Enlightenment, which had its roots in the scientific revolution was based on an emphasis on reason, and scientific methods and was advocating universal education and individual liberty in the name of progress. Being able to print books spread the new ideas rapidly.

Reformation from the Hungarian perspective

The wish to reform the corrupt Catholic church, to make the *Bible* accessible to believers through using the vernacular was already apparent in the early 15th century. The spread of Reformation and eventual victory throughout Europe triggered an increased reliance on the mother tongues, a secularization of learning, religious tolerance and the separation of church and state.

The Reformation

1409 – Huss becomes professor at Prague University, Hussite ideas (precursors of Reformation) spread over Central Europe.

1439 – First Hungarian language *Bible*, translated by two Hussite Hungarian scholars, who studied in Prague.

1517 – Luther posts his 95 theses on the door of Wittenberg Cathedral as a protest against Catholic Indulgences.

1519 – Luther declares Sola Scripta: scripture alone is the basis of Christian faith.

1522 – Luther publishes the *New Testament* in German.

1526 – Tyndale publishes *New Testament* in English.

1526 – Most of Hungary adopts Protestantism.

1529 – Zwingli starts Swiss reformation.

1534 – Loyola founds Jesuits as a counter-reformation move and re-converts parts of Poland, Hungary and Germany to Catholicism.

1534 – Henry VIII becomes supreme head of (Protestant) Church of England.

1536 – Calvin publishes his Theology (in Latin).

1541 – First Hungarian *New Testament* published, the first ever printed book in Hungarian.

1555 – Cuius Regio eius religio, which allowed the princes of states within the Holy Roman Empire to adopt either Lutheranism or Catholicism within the domains they controlled.

1611 – *King James Bible* published in English.

It is obvious looking at the timelines of Reformation that Hungary was well primed to accept the new ideas of Luther because of a hundred years' contact with the Hussite movement. By 1530, Mezőtúr wholeheartedly embraced the new ideology of the Reformation, particularly the wish to use the mother tongue in religion and education. The Ottomans were indifferent to the locals' religion, so Protestantism thrived.

In Mezőtúr the Calvinist-based humanistic,

tolerant, enlightened tradition continued unbroken for 400 years. However, at the end of the Second World War the school buildings were requisitioned and the priceless collection of books and instruments destroyed. The ethos of the school was not deemed to be aligned to communist, socialist principles. The teachers were dismissed without a state pension. My father had a pathetic letter from one of his old, much respected teachers. He was starving and ill. The 'old boys' helped, as much as they could.

With new staff the buildings were then used for a vocational college for agricultural machinery.

Such a sad parallel to Ignaz Reinbold's story. Institutions of learning, which stood the test of time for centuries and believed to be impervious to political changes, can and do suddenly disappear in a puff of smoke.

The Wooden Chest

The wooden chest, capacious and contented, now stands next to the bathroom holding odds and ends. In true Hungarian peasant style, it is decorated with bright red tulips on a blue background, with metal handles on either side.

It was not always so fanciful.

The Reverend László Gyüre, pastor of the 1500 or so Calvinist souls of Tiszaderzs, ordered it from the village carpenter in 1908.

He wanted the box, solid and long-lasting, for his younger son who was leaving for boarding school. The carpenter knew what the minister wanted; after all, he had made many such chests for other students and smaller ones for soldiers. The elder Gyüre boy, Laci, was similarly equipped not two years before. He made a fine job of it too, from good thick wood, dome shaped on top, so that it could be packed well, and painted it a very serviceable brown, for young Dezső.

For the next ten years this box would contain everything he owned and would travel back and forth from the dusty village to the famous, 450-year-old Calvinist school of Mezőtúr. Setting out into the big wide world, leaving the village the first time on a hired horse and cart for the nearest railway station, was a scared boy, my ten-year-old father.

His father took him on that memorable journey. He was not the only Calvinist minister accompanying his son. He met another eighteen village pastors there, on the same mission. The other new boys were sons of teachers, smallholders, tradesmen and businessmen. Among the lads there were quite a few Jewish boys too, the school accepted pupils from any religious denomination.

His box was packed with everything the school asked for and a bit of extra cake in case he got peckish. And his father gave him some spending money as well.

School started and the new pupils were told that they also had to buy some more things, such as rulers and books. Little Dezső diligently acquired all necessary items from the school shop and was shocked to find that his money ran out. By then he had some new friends, more worldly wise than himself, and asked one of them what to do. 'Easy,' said the mate, 'write to your dad and ask for some more.' Relieved by such an easy solution, he wrote a touchingly naïve but pithy letter:

Dear Father,
I have spent the money. Please send me some more.
Your loving son,
Dezső

The money came, by return of post, as well as a stern letter from his father, warning against the worldly pleasures of sweets in the shops and other unnecessary frivolities.

He must have been deeply hurt that his father could have supposed that he might have been careless. Even in his eighties when recounting the story, there was a tremble in his voice.

But the lesson was well learned and lasted a lifetime. I, as his daughter, can testify that never, ever was he comfortable spending any money on anything he considered mere frippery. And, as we all know, what a middle-aged gentleman and his growing daughters might consider 'mere frippery' are two very different concepts.

The student box returned to Tiszaderzs, the parental home in 1918, when he matriculated brilliantly and early from Mezőtúr, only to be called up, like all the four years preceding him. It was the turn of his year to join the army to fight for Hungary, to defend the Motherland and to end all wars. However the initial wave of excitement and optimism was well and truly over. Many of his previous schoolmates were now dead. My father did not wish to be killed. He decided the best way to escape was to be 'average'. It gave him great satisfaction that the drilling sergeant still didn't know his name at the end of the training. Peace was mercifully declared by the time he finished, and he never saw any action.

He applied to Budapest Medical School and was accepted. Even as a young boy he only ever wanted to be a doctor. Where to stay? Old Mezőtúr friends knew of a place, 144 Soroksári út; way, way out of town. It was built for the 1848 wounded soldiers, a bit like the Chelsea pensioners' homes in London. With just a few ancient survivors still living there, it was ideal accommodation. The building is long since demolished.

So the chest went to Budapest, together with its owner, to study medicine.

It wasn't easy in 1919. For a start, there was political unrest. Headed by Béla Kun, early in 1919 the Hungarian Soviet Republic was declared, instigated by Soviet Russia. Civil war ensued and more bloodshed. It was unwise for students to be out after sunset because the streets weren't safe. The Commune only lasted 133 days and my father managed to keep out of harm's way.

The economic collapse, the aftermath of the lost war, affected everyone, including my father. He was penniless, his mother widowed on a pitiful pension and all the money they had before the war was 'invested', never to be seen again, in War Bonds. But he was amongst cheerful friends. József Erdélyi, the famous poet, was one of them. They were young; they were hopeful, cheerfully destitute. No wonder he always liked *La Bohème*.

One of the lads (Lajos Szabó), went home to see his parents and they sent him back with a rucksack full of flowery potato cakes. You can imagine how this little anecdote will finish: by the end of the evening the rucksack was devoid of potato cakes. Lajos shared his treasure and the group of friends gobbled up the lot.

All he possessed was in that wooden box. He used to walk from his suburban digs, all the way on the endlessly long Üllői út to get to the university, even the tram fare was beyond his means. Food was also a big problem. By way of supper on his way back, he habitually bought a quarter of a pound of broken bits of pork scratching and whatever debris was left in the butcher's roasting tin. The owner came to recognise him as a not-too-profitable customer, and eventually greeted him loudly, in front of all the other shoppers: 'A quarter of sweepings for the gentleman!'

Yet he slogged on, even if he felt humiliated, all through the five long years of his studies and was singled out by the world-renowned Professor Heim to spend his last practising year in the prestigious Budapest teaching hospital, now called The Paul Heim Children's Hospital.

A year later he gained a scholarship to study in Berlin. He eventually obtained three different specialisms: paediatrics, urology and infectious diseases. His thirst for knowledge and looking for new connections accompanied him all through his life. At the age of eighty he still studied.

Much worn and ready for peaceful retirement,

the box snoozed quietly all through the roaring thirties, and well into the forties, in Tiszaderzs. Who would have thought that its greatest role was yet to be played? Yet it was this box which accompanied my parents, my grandmother and me, holding everything they had during their wilderness years, fleeing from the approaching front of the Second World War. I don't remember any of it.

After that, the battered brown box was always with my parents and stood in the corridor, its shabbiness modestly disguised by an embroidered cover. Spare goose-down pillows were kept in it now and I, as a six-, seven-, eight-year-old, used to curl up on it and read and read. It was my very own, private place.

It occasionally also contained treasure. Like some religious rite, the jam-, preserve- and pickle-making fever engulfed the whole of Hungary during the summers through my childhood. For weeks and weeks the season went on, starting with the early cherry compote, sour cherry juice and jam through to apricot and summer vegetables, finishing with late plums. The basic litany of: 'Fruit and sugar in equal quantities; boil in large saucepan; pour whilst piping hot into jam jars; add a sprinkling of "salicylic" powder; close with shiny wet cellophane; wrap in newspaper and place amongst pillows to cool for a day,' is etched in the memory of all my contemporaries.

High above us, the ominous clouds of the Cold

War, of political insanity, shifted, dispersed and gathered again. Down below, though, the nation chopped and chutneyed, peeled and pitted, sliced and shredded anything they could lay their hands on, as a national sport. The love of fine food, richly fruiting trees, and necessity – for there was nothing in the shops – and the close memory of starvation, all fuelled the fervour. The wooden box now had the honourable task of harbouring the delightful promise of good things to eat.

Meanwhile my father worked, studied and published scientific papers. He lectured at the Szeged Medical University. He lived his life methodically, undeviating, on a straight path, ignoring politics around him. On principle he never charged any patient for consultancy.

His grandchildren he would push on the swing with great good humour fifty times with his right hand and fifty times with his left. No more, no less. That was their ration, no deviation from it and everyone knew where they stood.

He devised a method too for how to be retired, at the age of seventy-five. Get up at 7 a.m., wash, breakfast, help his wife by doing the cleaning, go to the medical library at 10, home for lunch, in the afternoon type up his findings from the library, supper, followed by an evening walk. This worked splendidly for him, not quite so well for my mother who already had her efficient and effective cleaning routine. She could hardly wait for her 'novice' cleaner of a husband to take himself off to the library so she could reach into all those untouched corners without hurting his feelings.

It was early in March, in 1988 when my mother rang me, saying, 'There is trouble with your father.'

A sentence like that somehow conjured up in my mind something very naughty. If it were not unthinkable, it could have been a spree of shoplifting or the yelling of abuse at the neighbours.

'He died.'

It was not sudden; he had declined quietly and with dignity over a period of months and went to sleep peacefully. My mother hardly knew what she was saying, but that sentence still makes me smile.

He was laid to rest in the Szeged Calvinist cemetery. He was well prepared. He designed his headstone himself. Plain, warm-coloured red granite, with a symbolic tree of life, reaching up to heaven. The inscription so simple: Dr Dezső Gyüre, a doctor. He also chose the hymns he wanted. He stipulated that the notice of his death should only be announced after his funeral, so that nobody but the closest family could accompany him to his grave.

So there we were, a small handful of people, in the bright March sunshine, the sky was delicate, a translucent blue and the canopy of the old trees was just bursting into the lightest of green leaves. The air was filled with sounds, joyous tweets, calls and chirrups. We walked along singing, following the minister's black gown as it billowed in the gentle gusts and the skeins of Psalm 90, 'I trusted you my Lord from the beginning'[1] were caught and dispersed by the breeze, blending with birdsong.

There was no eulogy, just a humble request to God to look at him kindly. It was a beautiful homecoming.

And do you know what? In spite of his best efforts, a few of his closest colleagues still came, though unbidden, to express their love and respect.

After my father died, the house became so very empty. We visited my lonely mother whenever we could. All she made now were one or two jars of apricot jam, to please her growing grandchildren.

Not much need for the box, only old clothes, mementoes, debris of the past were all it contained. My daughter, Liz, and I had the idea to dress it up into a new, cheerful suit, to repaint it in the old farmer's style, with tulips and roses on a dark blue background and to make it happy. My mother and Liz's friend, Michelle helped too. So there it stands, in my own apartment now, next to the bathroom, masquerading as a genuine piece of antique painted Hungarian folk furniture. Is it a lie? I don't believe it. The outside says: I am Hungarian and can't be anything else. Its story also says: I have followed a uniquely Hungarian path through the past 100 years.

May it only see peace and prosperity from now on!

---

[1] First line of the Hungarian text.

One of the songs he selected was Psalm 90: *Prayer of Moses, Man of God*, and an anthem of Hungarian Calvinists. It was a very private and modest man's last and perhaps only clear declaration of beliefs.

I have only selected a few lines, those I know were important to him. Read it now, as if you have never heard of it before because it is truly beautiful.

Lord, thou hast been our dwelling place in all generations.

2 Before the mountains were brought forth, or ever thou hast formed the earth and the world, even from everlasting to everlasting, thou art God.

4 For a thousand years in thy sight are but as yesterday when it is past,

10 The days of our years are threescore years and ten; and if by reason of strength they be fourscore years, yet is their strength labour and sorrow; for it is soon cut off, and we fly away.

12 So teach us to number our days, that we may apply our hearts unto wisdom.

14 O satisfy us early with thy mercy; that we may rejoice and be glad all our days.

16 Let thy work appear unto thy servants, and thy glory unto their children.

17 And let the beauty of the Lord our God be upon us.

The Gyüre siblings, L to R: Dezső, Lenke, László, 1906. They wanted to go barefoot like other village children, but weren't allowed.

First job, in the children's ward in Pécs Hospital, 1926, Dezső on the left.

The love of his life, Ilma, 1942.

A very rare occasion, visiting Father in his consulting room, 1950.

With grandson Michael, at the playground, fifty times with the right hand... 1976.

The sun's going down, 1987.

Lampshade and Gratitude

1966

Let's go back to where this book started. It was 1966, I married David in Szeged, got my degree and the time had come to leave everything behind and start a new life in England. I didn't have much, but what I carried still amounted to a sizable luggage.

My mother came to the East Station in Budapest to see us off as we mounted the Vienna-bound train, to change there, catch the connection to Ostend, board a ferry to Dover, get a train to Victoria, then the underground to Kings Cross and finally another train to Cambridge. Not an easy journey, even if you just carry your passport in a slim handbag.

We stood on the platform; uneasy, somewhat awkward, for what is it you can say in the last ten minutes you haven't said before? And Mihály turned up. He was carrying a table lamp. Not just any lamp, he made it himself and it was his wedding present to David and me. He'd wired up a 19th century brass candle holder, made a lampshade from stiff paper, 'antiqued' with linseed oil to make it look like aged parchment, and covered it with copies of illuminations from the *Gesta Hungarorum*.[1]

Now if there is one thing you don't need on a lengthy train journey across Europe, it is an unwrapped and fragile lamp. Where do I put it? Is it safe on the rack? Can't go into anything, too big, too delicate, has to be held aloft and carried on its own. I still have an image of myself crossing the channel, up on the windy deck, clutching a candlestick with a large lampshade. I must have looked quite deranged.

The lamp, though, I loved. The mediaeval scenes were exquisitely painted, it gave a friendly light, (after the two pin plugs were exchanged) and it was given to us by Mihály. He was my uncle and he wasn't. My mother's parents were Béla Reinbold and Ida Muller. But Béla's sister, Ella Reinbold, married my grandmother's brother. So their two children, Mihály and Anita were cousins to my mother and her sisters. But since they were cousins from both sides, having the same four grandparents,

---

[1] The *Gesta Hungarorum* is the first ever surviving history of the Hungarians, written in Latin by an unknown scholar around 1200 at the request of the Hungarian king, Béla III. All we know about the author that his initial is P and he is always referred to as Anonymos.

genetically, they were siblings. They were all very conscious of this and the ties were very strong between them all. That was another reason I was pleased to see him at the station. I knew that my mother was very sad to see me go and Mihály's presence made our parting easier for her.

It wasn't the first time that Mihály just turned up from nowhere. Way back in 1944 during the siege of Budapest, Mihály appeared like a guardian angel to escort my grandmother and Alice across the Danube when he heard that the bridges were about to be blown up. He risked his own life to save theirs.

As a young man, Mihály was handsome with striking blue eyes, debonair, willowy and elegant. He studied law and worked as a diplomat in Vienna before the Second World War. Manners were certainly important to him. The family story goes that as a student he would place a mirror on the table while he ate in order to observe how he sat, how he held the cutlery, how he would reach for the cruet. By the time I knew him, well into middle age, he was definitely very polished. I remember admiring his languid grace as he would recline in an armchair, long, lean legs crossed, leisurely smoking his cigarette.

As he was a good few years older than my mother he was always 'big brother.' When I became a student in Budapest he automatically took on the role of guardian. Sometimes I would go to their home, to talk to Nora, his wife and their son little

Mihály, who at the time was still a small child.

As most students I habitually 'dined' at the mensa, the university-sponsored eatery for students, where food was very cheap, but correspondingly also an unappetising slop. Other choices included some kind of a bun, on the hoof, or a plate of chips in a fast food place.

The occasional invitation from Mihály for lunch was a real treat. He knew all the nooks and crannies of the capital and he chose with care, nice, little stylish restaurants or a 'picnic' of lovely bread, cold meats and dips in his office, which I liked even more. He opened my eyes to a different world, not the sober, strict, unadorned, studious Calvinist atmosphere of home but an equally honest, loving but relaxed and elegant world, where appearances and style also mattered.

All that showy elegance was only a façade. Beneath lay the real man, loyal, kind, resourceful with dogged determination and minute attention to detail. Being with him was as much an education as any of the lectures. If there are beacons in one's life, he was one of mine. Beacons, which say: look, have you thought of combining these ambitions with these attitudes? It was this blend which I admired: how to be sophisticated but not pretentious, how to have a clear moral code yet be non-judgmental.

Little did I realise that all this would be of great service to me. When I came to live in Cambridge an invitation to high table or a 'meet the Master for

248

sherry' didn't worry me, at least from an etiquette point of view, I knew how to behave.

It is curious, I hardly knew him before I was a student, but with contact I 'recognised' him. Think of an extended family as a series of dishes. The ingredients which made up my immediate family were all there, more of one ingredient, less of another, with slightly different spices perhaps but recognisable and comforting nevertheless. What his job title was, some kind of lawyer-ish thing, I never enquired about. (Oh the self-centred callousness of youth!) All I could see was a large sunny room, files, papers, telephone. Whatever he did, he must have been very good at it to have such a big office all to himself and he definitely was not a member of the communist party.

Big office or small office, in the '50s everybody was obliged to display Stalin's portrait. Mihály had a solution: he copied the ancestral shadow portrait and displayed it proudly in his office. It looked sufficiently Stalin-like to satisfy his superiors. This private joke, not without some danger, pleased him no end and he dined out on the story long after Josef Reinbold, AKA Stalin, disappeared from the wall.

This recognition of family traits included the Reinbold visual leanings. To be surrounded with things which are in harmony was important to him too. In his office I once saw a big, brown, floor-standing earthenware jug, with metre-long flowering spirea branches and tall blue irises. It was the most beautiful arrangement I ever saw. It surprised me, it wasn't effeminate, just stunning. He, like all of them could paint and make anything without any hassle. Copy an ancient codex? No problem! Recreate Stalin? What fun!

He was easy company. What's more, he liked David. On that last summer at home, when we were about to be married and things were somewhat fraught with getting all the necessary documents, David did not stay in my family home. My father arranged separate lodgings for him with friends. My father's argument was: 'David would not want it to be any other way.' And I thought: 'Oh, wouldn't he? It was the '60s after all. Mihály quietly and kindly offered his summer house to us, just in case we would like to see the Danube flow by.

He also had the same silent longing I recognised so well from my grandmother. He bought a plot with a little summerhouse in Surány on an island in the Danube to escape the congestion and noise of the capital. In hopeless futility he planted, in that sandy clay river soil, edelweiss, the almost religiously sacred flower of the far off Carpathians.

From this longing and loyalty stemmed his passionate interest in family history. It was Mihály who collected the old documents; it was Mihály who saved these irreplaceable treasures for us by sewing them into the lining of his winter coat and smuggling them through the border when Transylvania was no longer Hungarian. And it was

Mihály who, at the end of his life, donated everything to the Hungarian National Archive to ensure that the collection would be kept together, and remain a treasure for us all.

He didn't stop there; as a hobby, or more as a passion, he researched the family history with all the meticulous attention of a lawyer. And bored the rest of the family witless, it needs to be said. Not everyone shared his interest. Complicated genealogical tables were the result, tracing some lines way back to the 13th century. I was fascinated, so he gave me a copy too. Debts need to be repaid and with grateful thanks I acknowledge that without Uncle Mihály's help I could never have written half of the family history.

We asked him to be one of our witnesses at our wedding and our firstborn, Michael, was named after him.

Ida Kristyóri, *cc1880*, with her two older children, Jenő and Zoltán, Mihály's father, as a baby. Our grandmother, Ida, wasn't yet born.

Zoltán, Mihály's father, seated second left, in the army, May 1915. A postcard sent to sister Ida.

Little Mihály at the Adriatic, with his parents. It was a favourite holiday destination before the First World War.

The lost Eden. Mihály and sister, Anita, in Benedek on the Transyvanian estate, cc1910.

Mihály was a witness at my parents' wedding.

The two witnesses at my wedding: Miklós and Mihály.
L to R: My father, Miklós, Zsuzsi, me, David, Anci, my
mother, Mihály.

255

Josef Reinbold, AKA Stalin.

The lamp.

The Nature of the Universe or
The Law of the Conservation of Matter

1898 – Present

The law of conservation of matter states that matter cannot be created or destroyed, although it can be rearranged.

Those who wish to study the concept in greater detail could consult Nasir al-Din al Tusi (1201-1274), who first floated the idea, or go directly to Lavoisier (1743 -1794), who clearly formulated the law and therefore earned himself the title: Father of Modern Chemistry.

However, if you wish to do none of the above then just listen to my tale and it will clearly explain how the theory works.

My story unfolds over twenty years and has two strands, that of my father's brother, Uncle László, and my mother's family silver.

Once upon the time there was the family silver, such as platters, dishes, cutlery and decanters. They formed part of my mother's trousseau as her share of what belonged to generations before her. They meant the endless summers of childhood to her, spent with noisy cousins on the family estate in Transylvania. It meant the welcoming, rural ancient manor house and the fast-flowing icy mountain brook, dammed into a pool for the children at the bottom of the garden; the whirr of estate workers, villagers, servants coming and going, and indulgent maiden aunts sitting in the dappled shade of the veranda, each armed with a darning needle, picking the seeds one by one from redcurrants to be made into jam by cook.

When my parents had to flee from the approaching front in 1944, the silver was bundled up and carted with them and ended up in the Lager in Germany. It survived the war intact.

After the Americans took control of Germany, my parents were able to start the excruciating journey home to Hungary in the slow cattle wagons. Why they couldn't take the silver I was never told. I suppose they only had so much room in each wagon for every family and now they had my baby sister as well. As a last-ditch option my father asked a local farmer's wife, whom they hardly knew, to look after the bundle until they were able to collect it. She agreed and there the silver was left, while we returned safely to Hungary.

Post-war inflation in Hungary was followed by the harsh austerity of communist dictatorship;

trumped up charges, denouncements and persecution were everyday occurrences while the country was hermetically sealed off. No foreign travel, no communication was allowed. Those who had any kind of family connections to the West were singled out and punished. No way would my parents contact the now West German farmer's wife about the silver. By that time it did not seem to be that important either because my father was silently mourning his beloved, idolised older brother.

'Disappeared, presumed dead,' was the official verdict. László was everything my father was not, easy in company, elegant and worldly, but his name was never mentioned during my early childhood. We, the children, didn't know that he ever even existed.

His poor mother, alone in Tiszaderzs, continued her lonely vigil for her missing son, refusing to move, for if he were to come home how would he find her if she wasn't there?

She passed away without ever knowing what happened to him.

László was a soldier, through and through. Even as a child, he wanted to be a soldier. At sixteen, at the outbreak of the First World War, he volunteered, forgetting to mention that he was underage. The usual story, on both sides of the conflict, young men, boys only, fuelled by patriotism, eager for some 'action', carried away by slogans of heroism and visions of bravery.

Both parents went to get him back. But by 1916 off he went as a young commissioned officer and saw some bitter action, was wounded at the battle of Piave and would have drowned in the Po river, had not one of his comrades pulled him out, risking his own life.

You would have thought that, by the end of the war, he would have had enough, but no, he still wanted to be a soldier.

It puzzled me to think that the son of a minister and a brother of a doctor, both vocations dedicated to peace, helping and healing their fellow men, would find the army life attractive. But there is a connection.

At the root of the belief system of all these male Gyüres, there is a longing for purpose and a conviction that there is something higher than any one individual. Intensely patriotic, László also believed in honesty, order, discipline and acting for the greater good; and for him that meant being prepared to lay down his own life if his country demanded it.

He enrolled at the Ludovika, the Hungarian equivalent of Sandhurst, and studied law. He lived the life of a debonair young officer: he was sociable, a story teller, a natty dresser, with a fashionable bachelor pad in elegant Buda. He also knew that he was a 'good catch' and was somewhat playing the field, enjoying female company but never letting himself be tied down – everything my father was not!

By the time Hungary was involved in the Second World War, he was a much respected, scrupulous, impartial army judge.

He told me a story once, about an army pal of his. The friend was a general, and his son a junior officer. This young man was caught stealing, bringing shame to the family name. What could a father do in such circumstances? There was only one thing possible, said my uncle with approval: 'The father arranged the young man to be sent to the Russian front, where he was duly killed, and honour reigned in the family once more.'

By 1945 it was all over. We had lost the war, all sacrifice was in vain. The Hungarian army was defeated, effectively, by both the Germans and the Russians. In the total collapse of what once was an independent Hungarian state with its own army, at the last possible minute and in great secrecy, László managed to slip away and found refuge in Canada. None of the family knew anything about his movements. While his mother pined and his brother mourned, he was alive and well, even married, living in faraway Toronto.

Without a doubt he would have been executed as a war criminal had he stayed in communist Hungary. Of course he longed to send a message back home but knew enough not to, he would have endangered our lives, as any known connection to the West was severely punished.

Toronto, mid-1950s

The middle-aged man with the immaculate haircut mopped the library floor. He cut a vaguely foolish figure in his baggy, 1940s-style suit trousers, still with the sharp crease, slowly, methodically going about his business, not looking at the people around him. Nobody seemed to have noticed him either.

Even if he could talk to them, which he couldn't for he had not a word of English, he had nothing to say to any of them. What had he to do with the babble of young girls blossoming into bizarre peony flowers, with their many-layered wide skirts, narrow waists and cone-shaped bras under ridiculously tight jumpers, or boys who all tried to look like James Dean, copying his leather jackets, tight jeans and Brylcreemed quiff, each like an outlandish cockerel, puffed-up, crowing on top of the dung-heap?

What had he to do with their incessant, thumping, savage music, rock and roll, they called it, or images of the siren, Marilyn Monroe and that Elvis Presley, gyrating, his songs like dreams of steamy, unbridled sex?

The world had changed. Everything has changed.

László Gyüre, who once presided over life and death is now a cleaner in a library – and is glad of it. You have to eat. What use is a degree in the law of a country which does not exist anymore, in a language which nobody speaks?

Like a diligent day-time ghost, with military precision he silently cleans the toilets and sweeps the stairs. But come the evening the exile is not so hard to bear. He can go home to his Hungarian wife. Yes, he is finally married – to a good-looking divorced woman, who came to Canada in search of an easier life, with two grown-up daughters.

So now he has a family of sorts, lots of brown furniture, crystal vases, crocheted doilies, and he is almost himself again; talking, eating, and thinking Hungarian.

Once a week, though, the real László emerges. A bunch of old boys, timeworn Hungarian soldiers to a man, get together and talk late into the night over a glass or two of wine. In the fug of was, could-have-been and would-have-been, time disappears. They are home, men of action, men of decision again.

So time passed and the world turned round its axis once more. In 1956 the Hungarian people revolted against the Soviet occupation. Though the revolution was defeated, the regime changed and foreign communication once more became possible.

263

László dared to send word home to his brother that he was alive. By now his mother was dead. They never saw each other again.

Coming home for him as a political exile was still too risky but he mentioned that his wife's sister still lived in Budapest. My father was overjoyed, eager to meet this lady to embrace her, to hear all about her life, life in Canada, see the photographs. This was the closest he could get to his brother.

It transpired that one of László's stepdaughters was married and living in West Germany. By 1960 travel became easier and she regularly visited her Budapest aunt. So it came about that my parents asked her to find the silver, left in safekeeping in 1945, and bring it back to Hungary bit by bit.

No problem, everything was still there, as it was left, said the letter from this daughter. But somehow or other only a few pieces found their way back to my parents. There was talk of a kleptomaniac German mother-in-law, or was it a neighbour? We never quite found out what happened, but my poor mother never saw her precious stuff again. And she was sad about it. They survived the war, the exile, they were safe with total strangers; it was relatives who proved to be the danger.

There was no silver. But the post brought a baffling note, from the Budapest aunt, László's sister-in-law.

She and her husband were renewing their bedroom and a container full of their old bedroom furniture would arrive to our home next Tuesday. Unasked for, unwanted, it came. Two large wardrobes, two beds, two bedside cabinets, one dressing table, minus the mirror. Dark brown, heavy and rain splattered they were, delivered during a downpour. Hmmm.

Everything had to be rearranged to make room for them. Whilst shuffling furniture, my mother guessed bitterly that we were sent them because they were feeling guilty about the silver.

'Don't ever, ever say anything about this to László,' warned my father. 'They are the only family he has got. He must never know.'

Then he laughed and added, 'You see, there is proof that matter does not disappear. Sometimes silver turns into furniture.'

And that was the end of the family silver.

There is a bit more, way beyond Lavoisier's theory. From his cleaner's wages, my Uncle László sent me the money when I was studying English at Budapest to spend a summer term at Cambridge University. There I met a boy and that is how I came to live in England after we were married. And that is how he and his brother could finally meet in our Cambridge home. The alchemy of love turned silver into real gold.

I have kept the dressing table without the mirror to use for pot plants.

Uncle László, just eighteen, in the East Carpathians, November 1917.

Postcard to his parents from the Prague training camp for new recruits; László, second from right.
Message on the back: *If you can, please send some bread in a parcel. Feb 1917.*

Nothing to see here. The peaceful bank of the Piave in Italy, near Maserada. This is where on June 15th, 1918, he was badly wounded in battle and would have drowned had a comrade, risking his own life, not pulled him out.

Second World War, the distinguished army judge.

László and his wife in Canada, 1950s.

268

By Niagara Falls, a reunion of exiled Hungarian soldiers. László fourth from right.

After twenty years, the two brothers are together again in Cambridge. My father is showing a letter from one of their aunts who was a real Mrs Malaprop and caused much merriment.

269

Possessions

Sitting relaxed in a circle of friends we were talking about memories. 'Describe your childhood bedroom,' I was asked. Suddenly my world reeled. I stammered.

I was a six-year-old again. Somnambulant, I walked into the room and saw the simple table with the four chairs in the middle, now covered with a finely embroidered rustic cloth. This is where my mother sits at mealtimes; opposite her is my father's place, my sister and I between them. Opposite the door there are the two windows, both with thick, painted, folding wooden shutters for the night, keeping the heat in and closing out the occasional rattle of a passing horse and cart.

Between the windows there stands the antique chest of drawers, taller than I am. Its four drawers contain all the clothes we have. The bottom one is my father's, the next is my sister's and mine, then my mother's. The top, shallower drawer is for an assortment of things: scissors, sewing, pencils and pens for school. Bread and food coupons, important papers and the family money are at the back, all separated in neat boxes.

A crouching boy, looking at his hand, as if he just caught a frog, sits atop the chest of drawers. It is a lovely, green eosin Zsolnay porcelain figurine placed to the right, asymmetrically, yet in perfect balance in the space. 'Look,' said my father, 'it's August already and the sun reached the little statue!'

The boy glowed in the rays of the sun, the economic lines richly contradicting the scarab beetle-like metallic shimmer.

The stove is next to the door, tucked in the corner, with the coal scuttle next to it. An ugly, black, tall, dirty and dangerous place, we children don't go near it. To the left of the door there is just enough room to have one of the two settees, placed in an L shape, the other takes up the whole of the far wall.

Between them, squeezed right in the corner, is a child's slatted cot. These beds are clever, disguised as a settee in the daytime, if you fold down the backrest they become double beds, pull out the box from underneath and there is the space for bedding. My father sleeps on one, my mother and I on the other; my four-year-old sister is still in the cot with the end taken off.

The daytime look is enhanced by a row of muted red, grey and ivory rustic folk-weave cushions, and above my sister's cot the only picture: a framed and very funny reproduction from a French medieval

Book of Hours, a peasant with decidedly X-shaped legs in purple breeches sowing seeds in an emerald green field. Above my father's bed a bookshelf.

On leisurely Sunday mornings – while my mother cooked lunch – he would occasionally take down a well-used copy of János Arany, the Hungarian Wordsworth, and read some poetry; I watched him, with his very old fashioned bow tie, listening to the melody as words dropped one by one, clinking coins, precious and old, falling, falling, rolling in measured rhythm.

No wonder I was stunned when I was asked to describe my bedroom. Up till that moment it never occurred to me, and the startling realisation was so new that it made me stammer when I declared it: I DID NOT HAVE A BEDROOM!

We all lived in that one room, our other room was unusable in the winter. The irony was not lost on me either, though I doubt that my English friends would have picked it up. In Hungarian the phrase: 'He had no childhood bedroom' means uncouth, lacking in refinement. I did not enlighten them, in case they agreed.

So soon after the war we only had the barest necessities. Signs of goodwill, coming from afar, precious as lottery wins, helped the belief that we were not alone. These rare harbingers from distant lands arrived in the shape of parcels. There were three separate such occasions. My mother wrote in one of her letters to my father in 1948:

You'll never guess what happened yesterday! Mr Bakó arrived unexpectedly, bringing a large bundle of clothes. (Mr Bakó was our Calvinist minister.) *Whether he was pleased that we waited with Judit's christening until he was free or he knew about our difficulties with four young children, or he just thought us worthy, whatever his thoughts were, he arrived with some wonderful stuff. Apparently faith communities in America donated the clothes and he was asked to distribute them.*

I remember the event well. The clothes were piled high on the dining room table, Mr Bakó standing somewhat in the background and the four ladies: my grandmother, my mother and her two sisters around it, eager, excited, but still restrained. So great a treasure all at once, how can you choose? Because that is what they felt they had to do, let another family have joy too.

I know that my grandmother had something grey and woollen. I know that my sister Zsuzsi got an artificial white fur winter coat, which we immediately christened the polar bear coat. The rest I don't remember, except that there was a very, very, *very* beautiful girl's dress, white with little red roses all over it. I wanted that, so very much. Nobody asked me. Alas Anikó, my eldest cousin had the luck. Strange, how so slight a disappointment can last a lifetime.

However, when my own little daughter was born

Mrs Maine, David's (my husband's) supervisor's wife, gave her a little frock, white, patterned with tiny red roses, and finally the circle was complete.

We were already living in Kiskunhalas a couple of years later when a Red Cross notification informed us that they were transporting effects left in areas no longer belonging to Hungary. My father's two splendid, pigskin-covered club armchairs were duly delivered, part of a set he was rather proud to own way back, in Ungvár, in his bachelor days. My parents were very pleased to have them, and not just because they needed furniture; they took it as another sign that normality was slowly returning, and it also represented a connection with the past. What astounded me though was the accompanying large box of exquisite chocolates, the first I had ever seen.

Another eight years passed. This was now after the 1956 revolution, when communication outside the country was becoming easier. A Ukrainian painter contacted my father. When they were newly married they bought two works from the artist but when they had to flee they couldn't take them. As the painter was Ukrainian and remained there, my parents asked him to look after the paintings, saying that when the war was over they would come and get them.

No chance of that, as it turned out, but the artist tracked them down some fifteen years later and offered to send the paintings on to Hungary. The parcel arrived, the canvases were unrolled. Two large pieces, one of a peasant family, the parents, a babe in arms and two young children, the other five smiling children, all wearing Ukrainian folk costume. Vibrant colour, expressionist style, in the background a hint of pine forest.

We looked. Splendid works. My father frowned.

'They are not the same pictures that we left behind! There used to be just two children in the family and in the other one, only four children and much younger... Well,' he concluded, 'time has passed.'

Those two paintings have given me endless joy over the years.

As you see, I have first-hand experience of being the recipient of other people's charity. In dire circumstances these can prove to be life savers; in others, like the chocolates, they bring hope and sweetness into an otherwise very tough existence. As if someone reached out, put his hand on your shoulder and whispered: you are not alone, others do care. Neither is the experience forgotten.

That, now nameless, faceless American woman, who gave away her little daughter's cast offs, how could she know that the dress with tiny roses would become an enduring yardstick of beauty, kindness and inspiration in someone else's mind on the other side of the globe?

We can never be sure what the results of our

actions might be, but this does not mean that we should not try and do the right thing. There are endless pleas for donations; from so many urgent causes, it can be difficult to decide what is more important. It doesn't matter, just give. Share your possessions; share your money, knowledge, time or energy. Your reassuring touch on a stranger's shoulder will be felt in ways you'll never know.

I told the story of how my possessions came to be here as I looked around my flat. Generations came and went, each leaving some reminder of their existence. I saw turbulence and flight, followed by periods of peace, new beginnings, filled with hope and times of accumulation. I saw the ebb and flow of history washing forever, some cataclysmic tides throwing up debris, undermining shores, changing landscapes.

Starting with Ignaz, of questionable parentage, establishing a new dynasty in foreign lands, the theme is a recurring one. To arrive somewhere else, whether willingly or by force, to be strangers but still do your best, this seems to be the fate of nearly every second generation in my family.

And it hit me. The 'refugees', those others, whom we seem to have a blanket mental image of, you know, the suspect ones, who speak another language, whose customs are slightly different than ours, who knows, they might even be dirty, and their clothes are certainly ragged... IT WAS US! It was me.

It is amazing to gaze down on this long chain of people, and have the privilege of being able to get a glimpse of their lives. I am but one link in this chain, the chain of my family. I look at them and they seem familiar. All of them. Those I knew, those I have only heard talking about and those whose diaries and letters I read.

Is it because I know that they are kin? I felt pride in their victories and compassion for their struggles. I wanted to know what their hardships were and how they managed to overcome them. Another, possibly even more interesting question for me was how they fared in times of plenty; did position and power seduce them?

I found that they worked hard, they achieved and then they lost and gathered themselves together again, but, whether they were up or down, they were good people. They were rich in love and therefore could never feel deprived. That is what has been handed down through the generations, that is my real inheritance, not the possessions.

Is it just my family with this kind of story? It would be nice to say that it is my line, us, who are special, but it would not be true. In fact, none of us can say that the place where we find ourselves now is the place where our kind has been forever.

We, or our ancestors, at one point came here. We are all strangers, refugees, newcomers along the line somewhere. All we know (if you are reading this) is that we are all human. That is what connects us, although each one of us is a world, different from the other worlds.

Empathy allows us to guess what someone else is thinking or feeling but we can never know for sure. Just occasionally, very, very occasionally, we make a real connection to another human being; we touch each other through love or charity, to give it another name. Those are the moments which make life worth living.

Indeed the greatest of all is charity, in its many meanings and myriad forms.

Mother's fur coat is a pre-war treasure; Zsuzsi is modelling her 'polar bear' coat, which came from an American charity in 1946. She grew out of it, so they took the sleeves out, added them to the length, and inserted new, knitted sleeves. We are clutching our possessions, dollies Sara and Rozi, respectively.

Maternal grandmother, Ida Kristyóri, holding baby Ilma, 1917.

Some 65 years later, in 1983, Ilma, now a grandmother herself, is watching grandson Andrew, who is patiently waiting for his ice cream.

This is the real inheritance: five generations down the line, and the smile of love is the same.

Author's Note

It is May, 2020, as this book is going to press. I haven't seen my family for two months now, no visitors have come to my house in that time, and I haven't been anywhere either. I am not alone in my alone-ness. The whole world is in lockdown.

We are in quarantine, for a hitherto unknown virus, Covid 19, is rampaging round the globe, with deadly consequences. So far in the UK alone, over 30 000, a small town's worth, of people have lost their lives. No one knows when the epidemic might end. Our only defence is to lie low, practise social distancing, regularly wash our hands for twenty seconds, and hope.

We all know instinctively that the world is changing, but we have no idea what the post-Covid world is going to be like. So we hope.

We hope that what we are experiencing is a chrysalis state and maybe something beautiful, like a butterfly will emerge. We know that our pre-Covid, greedy caterpillar existence, devouring everything wherever we went, was deeply damaging to the whole Earth, and ultimately to ourselves. Maybe the Covid lesson is mankind's salvation.

The current, much used word in the media is

'unprecedented'. And in a way it is. We have never had a global pandemic on such a scale before. But there is nothing new in its effects. Panic, fear, uncertainty, shortages and death have always been mankind's 'travelling companions'.

Perhaps reading about my family's experiences, through similar cataclysmic events, can reassure us that we can get through all this. We don't know what the new world is going to be like but with hope and love we shall thrive again.

Ilma Scantlebury
Manchester
May 2020

About the Author

The scene of Ilma Scantlebury's childhood was the Great Hungarian Plain of endless skies, gentle rivers and lavish orchards. She studied at the Universities of Szeged, Budapest and, after she married her English husband, briefly at Cambridge and finally at Norwich.

Widowed now, her husband was a professor of Corrosion Protection at Manchester University. She has three children, and her working life has revolved around education, either in a teaching or in an organising, enabling capacity.

Printed in Great Britain
by Amazon

44431891R00175